Purchased in London
May 1979
Corinne Bordwell

SUFFOLK VILLAGES

Suffolk
Villages

ALLAN JOBSON

*Photographs by Peter Doubleday
the author and others*

ROBERT HALE · LONDON

© *Allan Jobson 1971*
First published in Great Britain 1971
Reprinted 1975
Reprinted 1979
ISBN 0 7091 2338 8

Robert Hale Limited
Clerkenwell House
Clerkenwell Green
London EC1R 0HT

PRINTED IN GREAT BRITAIN BY
CLARKE, DOBLE & BRENDON LTD.
PLYMOUTH AND LONDON

Contents

Author's note to 1979 printing

Since the last reprint of *Suffolk Villages* was issued a sad ravishment has taken place. Five villages in the north-east corner of the country, viz. Burgh Castle, Bradwell, Belton, Fritton and Hopton have been moved into Norfolk. The physical boundary line of the Waveney has been ignored by officialdom.

The fact remains these are essentially Suffolk settlements of the South Folk, and as far as this book is concerned the work of the planners is a non-event.

A.J.

Illustrations

Between pages 144 and 145

PICTURE CREDITS

Peter Doubleday: 1, 2, 4, 8, 13, 15, 16, 19, 20, 22, 24, 25, 30, 31, 32, 33, 34, 35, 38, 39, 40, 41, 43, 45, 46, 47, 48, 51, 52, 54, 55; The author: 3, 11, 12, 14, 21, 37, 44, 49, 50, 53; *The East Anglian Daily Times*: 5, 6, 7, 9, 17, 18, 23, 26, 27, 28, 29, 36, 42; P.A.-Reuter Photos Ltd.: 10.

SUFFOLK
VILLAGES

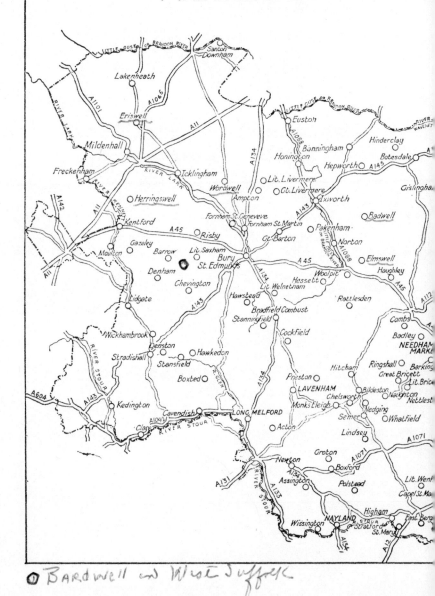

"If you would be known, and not know, vegetate in a village; if you would know, and not be known, live in a city."

CHARLES CALEB COLTON, *Lacon.*

I

Return to the Village

THIS little book is quite different. It is not a history of, or a guide to, Suffolk, but might be described as some 'Five Hundred Variations on a Theme of Peace'. Could one have a better subject? I do not think so, but one might have a better master of the muted music. Herein will be found no township, unless one creeps in unawares, being no less than a village in disguise. Such, for instance, as Eye, where a signboard of a muffin maker in Norwich, announced—"Patronised by Royalty, and the Mayoress of Eye". But rather little hamlets which our fathers thought were the most famous places on earth and would lament as though bereft of an only son when a tree was blown down, or felled by unholy hands. It deals with places that could produce an epitaph such as:

> Live well and die never
> Die well and live ever.

And:

> Where the long shadows of quaint yesterdays,
> Tempers to-day's fierce glare.

In some respects I am qualified to write these pages, because I am old enough to remember the magic atmosphere of that old world and its quality of light. When Queen Victoria died country roads and lanes were still country roads and lanes, with all their sleepy charm come down from countless generations, as G. M. Trevelyan has pointed out. Also, because the impact of delight and wonder came to me from outside. If I had been born in a Suffolk village it could hardly have produced this nuance, it would have been taken for granted and so passed unheeded. It was this wonderful passing from shade to light that made me not only a lover of Suffolk but a lover of the haunts of ancient peace. This thrill, this delectable experience, can be brought back even by a faded photograph, a scratched-out letter written by candlelight bearing a penny stamp, as well as by a Constable sky.

But how can I tell you of a peace that was audible, of the sweet-smelling savour of lanes that resembled some cow track leading from the field to the farm, as Hiliare Belloc described the main street of Lynn; or how the "drowsy tinklings" lulled the distant folds? The old life of the countryside blown through by the airs of heaven has gone, with those vast old hedges overrun with clematis, bryony and wild hops. That unhurried life of quiet pursuits, calm spirits and eternal gestures has passed. Yet the artlessness of daylight, the enchantment of the innocent eye, imparting wonder to all it beheld, remains, caught for us by a Suffolk artist, John Constable, who was the only one of his day who saw them or painted them in that particular way. It was another Suffolk painter, Gainsborough, who wrote that he was sick of portraits and was always wishing to take his viol de gambo and walk off to some sweet village where he could paint "landskips".

But we must remember it was not always thus, because Sir Philip Sidney had a word to say about it. "Nature never set forth the earth in so rich tapestry as divers Poets have done, neither with pleasant rivers, fruitful trees, sweet smelling flowers, nor whatsoever else may make the too much loved earth more lovely. Her world is brasen, the Poets only deliuer a golden." Which brings to mind what George Moore said of Corot: "he lay down and dreamed his fields and trees."

It is a curious fact that the coming of the railways, said to be England's gift to the world, began the drain from the village; and it is the machine that has become man's master (whereas the horse was his friend) that is driving him back again. This faceless juggernaut that hurls us across the world has filled hearts with fear, the fear of ultimate total destruction. It is the attempt at escape that prompts a man and his family to probe out and find the quiet spot, the "enchanted island in the sea of time", where he can find rest for his soul. After all, the village is ageless, towns may rise and fall, but villages, man's earliest settlements, go on and on, even though modern vicissitudes of roads, airfields, reservoirs, and the everlasting overspill would destroy it.

"Why does a virtuous man take delight in landscape? It is for these reasons: that in a rustic retreat he may nourish his nature; that amid the carefree play of stream and rocks, he may take delight. . . . The din of the dusty world and the locked-in-ness of human habitations are what human nature habitually abhors. On the contrary, lake, mist and the haunting spirits of the mountains are what human nature seeks." That was written by a Chinaman as long ago as the eleventh century, but might equally have been penned but yesterday.

The commuter is a quite modern phenomenon of the townsman. To anyone who knows anything of the human stream that passes over London Bridge in the mornings and again at night, or witnesses the eastward-bound Underground trains bearing their drear-hearted loads to their daily tasks, and the same trains westward bound in the evening, it is a sight really astonishing. They have but one song, "When I retire", or "When I can get away from it all!" Surely Trevelyan has summed it up: "An even more important consequence has been the general divorce of Englishmen from life in contact with nature, which in all previous ages had helped to form the mind and the imagination of the island race."

And again: "The men of theory failed to perceive that agriculture is not merely one industry among many, but is a way of life, unique and irreplaceable in its human and splendid values."

Yet the late Sir William Slater could address the agricultural section of the British Association at Norwich in 1961, stating that he saw the replacement of the old-time farmer by a company run by high-powered executives. Farming, he said, was no longer an art or a way of life, but a highly scientific business, and as such it called for highly scientific management. We can only hope that time will prove him wrong.

Which brings us to this happy county of the South Folk, with its astonishing variety, one little settlement differing from any other place in the whole world. Its insularity has been its guerdon, not only for the preservation of its own peculiar beauty, but according to Chaucer for the protection of his merchant:

> Would the see were kept for anything
> Betwix Middleburgh and Orwell.

It is divided from Norfolk by the Waveney and the Little Ouse, hence its erratic shape; and on the south the Stour through all its length parts it from Essex. Two little sweet singing streams of Lark and Linnet help to separate it from Cambridge. Lilian Redstone points out that the only path that linked this water-surrounded county with the rest of Britain was the Icknield Way, passing through Newmarket, crossing the Kennett at Kentford and the Lark at Lackford, following the boundaries of the Blackbourne and Lackford Hundreds to Thetford. Incidentally, when Edward Thomas passed this way a child came running up to him near Newmarket to ask if he had found a penny among the trees. He did not until afterwards suspect that this was a brilliant variation from straightforward begging.

At the time of the Domesday survey, Suffolk was divided into twenty-four hundreds, which became twenty-one in more modern times. At the Conquest it is said, excluding Middlesex, it was the most densely populated county in England. Moreover, the people were as remarkable for their quality as for their quantity. Of the 12,423 freemen recorded, 7,400, or more than half, were in Suffolk.

In this area many of the peasants kept poultry and ate the eggs, most had a plot of land with their cottage home, where peas, beans and more primitive worts were grown, and where sometimes a cow or pig was kept. The most important event in the time of Chaucer (1340–1400) was the break-up of the feudal manor, which led to the transformation of the English village from a community of semi-bondsmen to an individual society. In that century there were none of the rigid divisions between rural and urban, which have prevailed since the Industrial Revolution. No Englishman then was ignorant of all country things as we are today.

Passing down the centuries, Young, in 1794, placed Suffolk in the forefront of scientific farming. Then, coming to this very present year of the eleven-hundredth anniversary of the Abbey, Bury St. Edmunds, Lord Stradbroke, the Lord Lieutenant reminds us that "all around are to be found the finest husbandry and the highest class of domestic livestock and bloodstock known to the world".

This is confirmed in the announcement made by the retiring president of the Suffolk Sheep Society, that 1969 was a record year for exports of Suffolk Sheep—1,230 animals had gone to twelve countries. France topped the list by taking 886, and her buying team would be back in May or June 1970. He attributed the society's success in Europe to efforts of Suffolk sheep breeders to go overseas and meet potential buyers.

Then, in April 1970, came this: "Ninety-six Suffolk sheep are being exported to Hungary, the second batch to be sold to the 'Iron Curtain' country in just over two months. Nine rams were taken by lorry to Yarmouth to be sent by boat. Thirty-seven rams were exported to Hungary last year and a further 86 in January 1970, through the Suffolk Society".

This splendid farming and sheep rearing led to wonderful Suffolk industries, which sprang up in her villages. These rustic hamlets manufactured not only cheap goods for their own use, but special lines in luxury goods for the open market. The woollen cloth was manufactured as regards the main processes in the countryside, and the rapidly growing cotton industry was conducted in the cottages. Norwich disposed of cloth made in East Anglian villages.

When the Suffolks laid down their lives at Ypres, in that dreadful holocaust of 1914–18, they would have been unaware that the ruins of the Cloth Hall had bartered the wealth derived from their own village homes.

When George II (1727–1760) began to reign, manufacture was a function of country life. The 'manufacturers'—a term then used to describe not the capitalist employers, but the hand-workers themselves—inhabited ordinary villages, each of which supplied its own clothes, implements and buildings of the commoner kind, as well as its own bread and beer. Indeed it was said that the cloth industry was destined to transform the social life of the country. It might be said in passing that some of this was due to the arrival in 1336 of a large number of Flemish weavers (displaced persons, old style). So that Lavenham became famous for blue cloth, Sudbury for baize, bunting and shrouds, Kersey and Lindsey for kerseymeres and linsey-woolseys.

Undoubtedly this led to the wealth of certain Suffolk families whose names are perpetuated to this day in London streets, such as the Drurys, Berners and Seckfords. Sir Thomas Gresham built the first Royal Exchange of Battisford oaks during 1566. The trees were cut down on his estate, the framework erected on Battisford Tye, marked with the old Roman numerals and sent to London, possibly by water. The Royal Exchange was opened in January 1568.

If these men of substance had a town house they had also one at home, so that Suffolk villages have many Elizabethan mansions, or more modest houses built in Tudor or early Stuart times. A sheer delight to mind and eye, with timber and brick nogging— brick having come back into England in the fifteenth century— and with those intriguing overhangs. These were England and home to the small gentry and yeomen free-holders who had supplanted the feudal nobility. And it was in these houses that could be found the elements of good living, to wit: "A fair garnish of pewter on his cupboard, three or four feather beds, so many coverlets and carpets of tapestry, a silver salt, a bowl for wine (if not a whole nest), a dozen of spoons to furnish up the suit." Or: "Usually he dined off pewter, but he had a silver dish, six silver cups, and some fine earthenware, and linen for festive occasions." Even the cold catalogue speaks of spacious, even gracious days in the village scene.

To this very day these ancient dwellings of our ancestors stand high amongst the homes and gardens of England. It is proudly announced that Suffolk will be among the leading counties in the number of private gardens open to the public. Among them are Redisham Hall, the Georgian house near Beccles, Hemingstone Hall near Ipswich, Knodishall Red House, Primrose Cottage and Saltlick, both of Southwold, and Ashe Abbey House, Campsea Ashe.

The last-named adjoins a fifteenth-century mill with its original machinery and a thatched barn, one wall of which is thought to have been part of the twelfth-century abbey. The house itself has twelfth-century timbers and a hammer-beam roof.

One of the most interesting West Suffolk gardens is that of Gifford's Hall, the moated fifteenth-century house at Wickhambrook. Others include Little Haugh Hall, Norton, near Bury St. Edmunds; Plumpton Hall, Whepstead; Bridge Farm, Brent Eleigh; The Priory, Stoke-by-Nayland, and The Lawn, Walsham-le-Willows.

Really, this is only natural, following a pattern set by the Tradescants, the Caroline gardeners who were natives to our East Coast villages. It is not surprising, therefore, that this appeared in the *Daily Telegraph* of 15th April 1964:

> America wants her daffodil bulbs back. Two experts from the Ministry of Agriculture went into a garden at Walberswick, East Suffolk, yesterday, took up samples of soil with a tiny trowel and put them in a plastic bag.
>
> The said sampling was the first step in obtaining an export clearance for an old-fashioned 'Daffodowndilly', known to botanists as the 'John Tradescant' daffodil. Tradescant was a 17th-century botanist who brought the golden, many petalled American daffodil back with him after a visit to Virginia. He planted some of his bulbs at Walberswick, where the family lived. Now people in America where the flower has been extinct, have asked to have some specimens sent over. Miss Mea Allen who owns the garden, said, "We call them Rose daffodils because they have a full centre like an old-fashioned cabbage rose. The Americans have arranged the import permit, but these formalities have to be completed."

The Tradescants, travellers, naturalists and gardeners to Charles I and Charles II, introduced into this country the Algerian apricot, the lilac, acacia and the Occidental plane.

Beyond all that, Sir Joseph Hooker, the eminent botanist and traveller, was born at Halesworth in 1817. He later became a friend and fellow worker of Darwin. His father, Sir William Jackson Hooker (1785–1865), while at Halesworth commenced bringing together the most extensive herbarium accumulated in any one man's lifetime. Both father and son became directors of

Kew Gardens. And, remember, there is a pub and a meadow known as 'The Pot of Flowers' at Stowmarket.

Suffolk was the home of long tenures, with names derived by patrimony, such for example as my mother's family of Barham. True, my great, great grandfather, Samuel Barham, does not appear in the registers of Middleton-cum-Fordley before 1799, yet he must have arrived from a nearby village, probably Yoxford, where the Barhams were of armigerous stock. He had issue eight children who populated Middleton in the nineteenth century, whereas now none remain. They spoke the language and followed age-old customs.

> In ford, in ham, in ley, in ton,
> The most of English surnames run.

Janet Becker, whom I knew, daughter of Harry Becker, the Suffolk artist, gives some good examples of these in her booklet on Wenhaston. She says that the Suffolk dialect is so unmistakable (a little incomprehensible to the 'furrina') that Suffolkers find friends wherever they go.

An old lady from Wenhaston staying in London for King Edward's coronation, found herself on a crowded street island. Turning to a policeman she said, "Sir, put us across." "Wait you a minute," he replied as the people hurried to the pavement, "give us yer hand, good old Suffolk." The old lady thought it was the intonation of her voice he recognized, but surely it was the typical phrase "put us across".

If romance and dialect go together, they undoubtedly mingle in the incident told me by a friend of the girl concerned. She had left her village not far from Wenhaston, to go out to service in London. One night she and a fellow servant went to an entertainment. They walked home talking about it. Presently they were aware of a young man following them, and, despite their dodging in and out, he kept close behind them. At last the girl turned on him. "Sir, I don't like being followed about." "Miss, I must apologize," was the reply, "you were talking. I couldn't help hearing—and I too come from Suffolk."

They walked out that Sunday, and were happily married, returning to live not far from Wenhaston.

Janet also instances some folk-lore. To roll one's soap between the hands instead of using it flat, insures one against marrying a land labourer. A girl who was known to practise this married a shepherd.

Such a Friday, such a Sunday.

When a kitten frolics about it is playing up rain.

Because a thunderstorm was raging on the night in June, many years ago, when a murder was committed in a neighbouring village, a storm is supposed to take place in that month every year.

Brides consult the old wedding rhyme:

> Monday for Health.
> Tuesday for Wealth.
> Wednesday best day of all.
> Thursday for losses.
> Friday for crosses.
> Saturday no luck at all.

"Friday for crosses" has perhaps arisen from the fact that the Crucifixion took place on that day. Mr. Francis Groom said that Suffolk had the distinction of having produced by far the best versions of the old folk lore then collected in England.

"Return to the Village," we see it in every issue of the morning paper, reporting events in the sale-rooms and the scramble for antiques and examples of home as lived in the peaceful days of our grandparents. One such is the work of Thomas Smythe, a painter of the Suffolk scene, especially Suffolk Punches, whom the 'trade' has discovered in the last few years. From absolute obscurity his work has risen to almost astronomical proportions. In 1968 "Cottage by a Pool" fetched £550; then "Duck Shooting in Winter" fetched £800 at the same time. Two studies of fisher folk on the shore went for £450 and £360, respectively. But in January 1969 one of his works, "Horses in a Country Lane", was secured for only £110. In March 1970 in an Ipswich sale-room a picture by him realized £1,250. Why? one might ask. Is it not but another attempt at getting away from it all, a return to the real life of simplicity that the countryside affords, a panacea for the stress and strain of modern life.

It has been said there was no uniform pattern among old windmills, of which there was usually one in a village, introduced into England at the time of the Crusades. Neither is there a uniform pattern in a Suffolk village, each one different, and each one offering something of peculiar interest in itself, as it rambles on to join the next.

That great observer of the countryside in his day, William Cobbett, said: "The land is generally as clean as a garden ought to be; and though it varies a good deal as to lightness and stiffness, they make it all bear prodigious quantities of Swedish turnips; and on them pigs, sheep and cattle all equally thrive. I did not observe a single poor miserable animal in the whole county." After remarking the "great number of farmhouses", and the cottages clean and comfortable, he did not observe "one miserable hovel in which a labourer resided".

This is what William White wrote in 1865:

> The scenery is quiet; gentle undulations, sprinkled here and there with copse and plantation, great breadths of grain for many a mile, presenting you with such a picture of Suffolk as would meet your eye in any part of the county. . . . For signs of rural ease and plenty there is no part of our island that contents the eye so fully as East Anglia; and there is withal so much that denotes settled habitation and long possession, as if the same homesteads had been inhabited by the same families ever since the days when the monks of Bury pruned their vines and harvested their barley. "We were here before the Conquest, and here we are now," might still be said by certain dwellers in Suffolk.

It must be realized that the people who populate the villages today are not those old families who were there for generations. They are fast dying out, hence the closure of the chapels, and their place is being taken by retired folk, service or otherwise, who have a resolute determination to return to Nature. They are keen enough, and decidedly on the alert for village rights, which surely is all to the good. In many cases they are bringing new life into old walls. This has been very evident in the exhibition staged by the Royal Institution of British Architects in this Conservation Year of 1970. One cannot be too thankful for this and the wonderful work of the Rural Community Councils and the Women's Institutes. Suffolk villages are to some extent maintaining their own, but the enemy is at the gates, and those adjacent to the towns are in a dangerous position.

Many of the villages may fairly be said to nestle into the country scene. From the distance the church stands out clearly and distinct, but on reaching the settlement of houses it often completely disappears and is hard to find. This is due to the heavily wooded nature of its surroundings, and to the gentle declivities of the landscape.

I suppose the greatest changes that have come to village life in recent years have been electric light and piped water. The latter has broken an age-old link with the past, through well or pump, around which a great deal of comradely feeling has always existed. The inconvenience of carrying pails of water considerable distances has been taken for granted, while the widow woman who lost a pail down the well always gained the sympathy of the whole village. However, when a neighbour came home after a day's toil, he would soon come to the rescue; creepers would be lowered and the pail retrieved. I would therefore refer you to the Suffolk riddle.

> As round as an apple,
> As deep as a cup,
> All the king's horses
> Can't pull it up. (A well.)

As to light, gone are the tallow candles and the rushlights, the latter having been made by my mother in her youth; as also the soft light of the paraffin lamps. They also were taken for granted, but were a pernickety problem in clean lamp glasses and trimmed wicks.

> If little gals goo an' play with the tinder,
> Why they fly all on fire and be burnt to a cinder.

Gone too, in so many cases, has the kettle on the hob. "Red Boy, make Black Boy's inside wobble." (Fire and Kettle.) A fire-place in the old days was usually referred to as a 'hob', and if renewed for any reason it would be: "Are yew a' havin' a new hob?"

> The cosy fire is bright and gay,
> The merry kettle boils away
> And hums a cheerful song—
> I sing the saucer and the cup;

> Pray Mary, fill the tea-pot up,
> And do not make it strong.

As a companion piece to the Church, is the village pub—so many of which, in my opinion, are of ecclesiastical origin, coming down from monkish days when the brothers brewed the beer. Some of these with their colour-washed exteriors still have a thatched roof; but it would be impossible today to find one that brewed its own beer. You would not even be able to find one exhibiting a gentle reminder to its clients, written in the true idiom, that it gave no tick.

> The brewer doth crave
> His money to have,
> The distiller say have it i must
> So good people you see
> How the case is with me
> In this tap-room i never can trust.

Or:

> To pay my bills you know
> That makes me careful who I trust
> Chalk is useful, say what you will,
> But chalk won't pay the Brewer's bill.

If you bought your tobacco there, you would get a pipe free in which to smoke it, and perchance a biscuit to mumble with your beer.

> Little tube of mighty pow'r
> Charmer of the idle hour
> Object of my warm desire
> Lip of wax and eye of fire.

We might include in this section a specimen of the county's humour.

One evening a noise was heard in the back kitchen of a Suffolk country house. The master went to see the cause, when, to his astonishment, he saw a man with a lantern in his hand, coming in

"Whatever do you mean by coming into my house?" cried he, going on to pour forth a flood of reproaches in language not mild by any means.

At last the intruder called out, "Ha' yow done?"

"Yes, I have," was the answer. "But I ask again—what are you coming here for?"

"Courtin' yar cook," cried the man.

"Courting my cook!" roared the màster. "Well, but what have you got a lantern for? When I went courting I never took a lantern."

The intruder slowly spoke with a broad grin. "Noo, I don't wonder at yow not takin' noo lantern along o' yow. I ha' sin yar missus."

Village feuds have vanished with village customs. These were the outcome of strong clannish feeling, expressed perhaps in rather a bucolic fashion. For example, Westleton men were great stone throwers and would combat with Middleton lads. Kirton men were fighters and would journey forth to do battle with adjacent villages. One supposes that football teams find an outlet today for this kind of local spirit.

The general shop must not be left out, although the old-fashioned variety is hard to find. The stream-lined primitive version of the would-be super-market has taken its place.

Neither may we forget the lovely old cottage gardens. How beautiful they were and are, with a fuchsia growing under the window, blowsy old roses begotten many gardens ago, and Mrs. Simkin spreading all over the place. How sweet they did smell to be sure, and what a glory was theirs.

Considering that Suffolk has some 500 villages, the exigencies of space will not allow of naming them all. But I must apologize in advance for the admission of so many superlatives in the text; such is local pride.

One thing more: it is constantly averred that Suffolk villages, and the county as a whole, are unspoiled. This must be taken in a relative sense, since village life is entering upon a new phase of growth.

2

The Villages of North-east Suffolk

At the first wink of the Morning Star let us wend away
To the frore fields, while the morning is young, the meadow pearly,
And dew so dear to cattle lies on the tender grass.

Virgil.

IN treating the villages, the old hundreds have been followed as far as possible. This serves to group them together better than the alphabetical method—although in some cases a somewhat jumbled picture as to location is portrayed.

The villages of North-east Suffolk comprise a very large number, yet only three of the Anglo-Saxon hundreds are involved. They include the Sandlings, which is really a counterpart of the Brecklands in the west. Moreover they include a good slice of Roman Suffolk, not only as it affects the coastal defences, but the inland routes from Colchester to Caister by Norwich. In short it is the most historic part of the county.

We might start the survey with Gunton in the extreme north, where the clay was dug that made the Lowestoft China, A. V. Steward in his *Lowestoft* says: "It is probable that the kiln was placed near the Warren Cottages on Gunton Denes. Here the spring would provide water for washing the clay, and there is also mention of an overshot water wheel. However, the picturesque Warren Cottages were demolished during the late war and only the spring remains to give point to the conjecture."

Jealousy and intrigues stopped the venture, it was thought, by the Bow China factory, or another London firm fearing a rival compe-

tition. But it was finally carried to success by a company of craftsmen and artists. Only recently have the last traces of the old kilns
disappeared. The venture flourished until 1803, producing 'Trifles
from Lowestoft' and birthday plaques duly inscribed. These were
sold to fisherfolk for a shilling or two.

This part of the county is the area of the round towers, a peculiar feature of building confined almost entirely to East Anglia,
with some 125 in Norfolk and 42 in Suffolk, and only 13 in the
rest of England. They have been an enigma to archaeologists, and
so remain.

Like their counterparts in Ireland their origin is obscure, but it
has been generally agreed, by those competent to judge, that they
are considerably older than the churches of which they now form a
part. Their antiquity has been naïvely suggested in the delightful
explanation of earlier 'natives', that they are relics of the Flood.
When the water subsided, it is said, these ancient well-casings were
left when the soft earth was washed away.

Dating from Saxon times they were probably used as strong-
holds, or lookouts against invaders. This theory is largely founded
on the fact that they are all to be found by water-courses, or what
was once a water way, as the one at Frostenden. They have no
staircases, and at one time, no tower arches. Where these latter
have been cut, the work has been of a later date. Neither had they
any openings at their lower levels, save slit-like windows. They are
most numerous in Lothingland and its immediate vicinity, suggestive of a watch over innumerable inlets at one time here so
much a menace. Others follow the Waveney, while yet others
are met within the winding ways of the Blyth. From the main
centre in the extreme north-east of the county they spread, exactly
as the Danish place-names of the eleventh century, along both the
coast and the river Waveney.

They are more or less of uniform size, varying in their diameters
at the base, with walls 4 feet or more in thickness. The reason of
their shape is probably to be found in the absence of local stone
for the quoining. But the fact remains that the mortar, into which
the flint rubble of which they are built is embedded, is as hard
and impervious as the flints themselves. Various speculations have

been rife as to how this was mixed, the suggestion being that white of egg was used. This is undoubtedly but a wild fancy; certainly, if so, eggs must have been in plentiful supply to provide such an ingredient. Their ancient builders knew how to build, not for an age but for all time. When a modern generation essayed to rebuild the tower at Spexhall that after a thousand years had collapsed, they found a good many problems as to foundations and, not least, expense.

An interesting fact was brought to light when the tower at Eccles, in Norfolk, was blown down in 1895. The blocks of masonry revealed a wheatstalk-like construction. It was evidently built in sections of about 10 or 12 feet. Each portion was perfectly smooth where broken off in the fall, as if the builders allowed one portion to finally settle before another was added. This is mentioned by Claude Morley in his monograph on circular towers.

Carlton Colville has a very interesting circular moat near the Bell Inn. It is one of those early earth works set deep in time, and is known as 'The Mardle'. It goes back to the days when Danes and Saxons fought for supremacy, and is thought to have been used as an enclosure for cattle to protect them from marauding bands. Later it was used as a parking place for drovers on their journeys. It may also have figured as a retting place for flax, when the hemp-lands were a necessary feature in rural and Poor Law economy. This process gave off a rather nasty smell. 'Mardle' is described by Forby as "a pond near the house, in the yard, or on the neighbour-ing green, or by a roadside, convenient for watering cattle". But it has another meaning in Suffolk, and that is to gossip. Can it be that these bits of water were meeting places where folks mardled in more senses than one? This bit of moat-enclosed meadow was also known as 'The Old Osiers', and certainly marks an ancient piece of Suffolk, as of England. Alas, it has developed into a rubbish dump, the moat has been drained and the site is likely to be built upon.

Carlton signifies the village of a husbandman, while Colville was obtained from a Norman family. One of these was of such a grasp-ing nature that he not only wanted all the earth he could get hold of, but the sky as well. He was Sir Roger de Colville, and when

Edward I came back from the Holy Land he was brought to book.

We have gone downhill too fast, so we will return to Belton. The round tower of the church has been re-built and looks like it. Inside, however, are some wall paintings, described by Dr. M. R. James as the Three Dead or the Three Living, retouched. Certain figures on the left do not seem to belong to the scene. Below it appears the legs and a fish of a St. Christopher. There is also a picture of St. James the Great.

It is not a great step from here to Burgh Castle, the best Roman building in Suffolk, and one of the best in England. Here was the Roman Gariannonum, and its immense walls and bastions speak in no uncertain manner of builders who fortified a difficult place with the strength that we could achieve today only by means of re-inforced concrete. It is primitive construction in its most impressive form, built, it is said, by the Roman General Scapula. The flint rubble is set in mortar that is still hard and impervious. Red tiles act as alternate courses with the rubble. This may have been the head-quarters of the Count of the Saxon Shore and the Stablesian Horse. In any case it dominates the confluence of two important rivers.

The church of St. Peter has a round tower from the top of which, so writes Suckling, "seventy churches besides Norwich cathedral can be seen with the aid of a telescope; most of which with the assistance of a map have been identified". In 1403 it was stated: "The Rector of Burgh church, Dean of Yarmouth, keeps and maintains fornicators in the town, taking of them bribes, and does not correct them. Fined 40s."

Bradwell round tower is pierced by circular windows, but is not so tall as some of the others. Within, the church is an interesting monument to William Vesey, Esq., which Suckling stigmatizes as being in the barbarous taste which prevailed at the commencement of the seventeenth century. He goes on: "In the lower compartment are seen four kneeling effigies, and a fifth, representing a child lying on its side. Village tradition relates that this group portrays the discovery by his four sisters of an infant brother, who had strayed from his home and was lost in Bradwell wood." What a happy little conceit, whereas the child succumbed to infantile mortality.

Fritton has been described as remarkable, this for two reasons—its beautiful lake known as Fritton Decoy, and the tiny thatched church. The latter consists of a round tower, a nave and a Norman chancel, which is the most interesting thing about it. The east window is in alignment with the tower, and not with the west end of the nave. One has to go down into the chancel which has an apsidal end, curiously groined roof and narrow slit windows that originally contained portraits of saints. It is something which should not be missed as a combination of styles and antiquity. "On the 17th day of August, 1816, Hannah Freeman did penance in the church for defaming the character of Mary Banham, spinster."

Herringfleet, on the borders of the two counties, has a church standing on what must have been once upon a time a strong defensive position. M. R. James describes it as an old little round-towered church where parsons are never instituted. However, this tower is very early Norman, with baluster windows, similar but not so fine as nearby Haddiscoe, which is in Norfolk.

Eastwards of the church stands a fine example of a barn once the refectory of the Augustinian priory. Bricks and pebbles provide alternate courses for this old thatched building, and present a happy and unusual effect of diapering; a lasting tribute to local genius. There was, or is, a colony of the lesser or pigmy shrews here.

Suckling gives an excellent and quaint account of what we should term escalation.

St. Olave's bridge, which crosses the Waveney near the site of the ruined priory, superseded a ferry which existed here at a very remote period. Before the reign of Edward I this ferry was kept by one Sireck, a fisherman, who received for his trouble bread, herrings, and such like things, to the value of 20s. a year. After his decease, William his son, did the like, and made it worth 30s. a year. Ralph, his son, also did the same, and had of his neighbours bread and corn, and of strangers, money. And because the prior of Toft hindered passengers from going through his marsh, the said

Ralph purchased a passage through the prior's marsh, paying 12d. a year: and of the commoners of Herringfleet, he purchased a way through their common, and was to carry them over at all times free for it, and then it became worth £10 per year. After Ralph's decease, John, his brother, had it, and it was valued at £12 per year. John sold it to Robert de Ludham, who made it worth £15 per year.

The church at Lound has another of the round towers. As at Blundeston, there is a curious circular hole $5\frac{1}{2}$ inches in diameter in the west wall of the nave to the north of the tower, which may have been a squint towards the altar. This was one of Suffolk's rich livings.

Suckling once again has a note of interest culled from the *Gentleman's Magazine* concerning discoveries of antiquities made in 1776 by William Warner Mills, whilst ploughing in his field in this parish. Amongst warlike objects several ingots of gold were turned up, which the farmer regarding as pieces of rusty iron used as weights for the purpose of sinking his hemp in the adjoining stream, where they were gradually lost with the exception of one. This, after having been long thrown about as a useless piece of lumber, was one day broken by an accidental blow, when the yellow and glittering surfaces of the fracture betrayed too late the value of what had been lost.

Somerleyton is chiefly noted because of its Hall and the families who lived in it, some of whom were "a little posterior to the Norman Conquest", as the old writers put it. That must have been a very comforting thought to those to whom it applied. A Jerningam built the hall, and the family ranked high among the most ancient in England. It then passed to the Wentworths, the Petos, and so on to the Crossleys. All sorts of interesting little bits could be written about it, including the north parlour, at one time converted into a billiard room, the table in which was framed out of portions of the wreck of the ill-fated *Royal George*.

Dear old Fuller, in his *Worthies*, ranked it "amongst the many fair houses of the gentry of this county. Sommerly Hall, nigh Yarmouth, belonging to the Lady Wentworth; well answering the name thereof: for here Sommer is to be seen in the depth of Winter, in the pleasant walks beset on both sides with fir trees, green all the year long, besides other curiosities".

At the coronation of Charles II, they collected £2 0s. 9d. for a bonfire, as recorded in the church registers, which was celebrated on St. George's Day 1661. To this Lady Anne Wentworth subscribed 10s., Ann Berry 6d., Mr. Starston "an hundred of faggot wood, John Aldrich a quarter of firs, John Everard the same, Robert Hayne of Herringfleet also, John Woolsey, a quarter of broome, John Dale a load of bones". The question arises, where did John Dale get the bones from?

Then follows "two barrels of beer, 9 duzzen of bread for the poor, tobacco, pipes, pruens [why prunes?], sugar, and for a carpenter to make a booth, and for one to watch it at night, one shilling". So they had a merry time. Somerleyton is that rare thing, a completely intact unspoiled village, with thatched cottages, village green, parish pump; and never a new house or bungalow in sight. People are proud to have been born there—"Why, my grandfather, a master plumber, was fitting a new clack to the old pump when he died. I never fail to go back at least once a year, because I love it so much." All this, because of Somerleyton Hall who owns the lot and keeps it as a sacred trust. And in those lovely gardens is a maze—easy to find the entrance but difficult about the exit. Bronze Age implements were dug up in the rectory garden in 1926.

Ashby is distinguished by its church tower, which is of considerable interest. The suffix 'by' is of Danish origin, probably bestowed on this place by settlers from that country who found refuge in these parts. The church stands on what appears to be an ancient way, now considerably removed from modern roads. The tower has a round base that turns to an octagon, the angles of which are brick-quoined, giving it an unusual and interesting appearance.

Oulton church, originally Norman, has a central tower. Its one-time magnificence is stressed by Suckling. "How imposing must this chancel have been in earlier days, when its painted oaken roof displayed the rich heraldic bearings of the Fastolfs and the Bacons, which occupied each boss and 'coin of vantage', while the

Two round-towered Suffolk churches: *(above)* Fritton and
(below) Thorington

Bramfield church with its detached round tower

Cockfield Hall gatehouse, Yoxford

Framsden Mill

Cookley Church Farm

Crow's Hall, Debenham

deep tinted glass, sparkling with the like achievements, poured
floods of light upon its sculptured fittings, in stains of varied
mellow lustre." On the front of the gallery hung the rather rare
Royal Arms of James II, which Suckling says came from St.
George's, Hanover Square, London. The magnificent brasses formerly here were stolen in 1857.

Naturally enough it is the Wherry Inn that holds its sign aloft,
because Oulton has one of the Broads. This brings to mind the
old keels and wherries that sailed quietly by with the answering
calls of "There ye go", "There ye sail! There ye lay! There ye sit!"
or "There ye shove! There ye blow, my love!" with "Here we go,
master!" The keel was entirely supplanted by the wherry, which
in turn has been supplanted by the cabin cruiser.

George Borrow, through his marriage with Mary Clarke—
daughter of the vicar, the Reverend Francis Cunningham—who
had been left a widow after a married life of only eight months,
entered into her dowry which included an estate on the north-
west shore of Oulton Broad. The house was known as Oulton Cottage, and it was an octagonal summer house, still standing, that
he made into a study where he wrote some of his books. His
friendship with the gypsies, who were encouraged to camp on his
estate, was never understood by his neighbours. Neither was his
morose and irascible disposition. It is said that on one occasion
he rode his horse up the steps and into the hall of Dr. Ray's house
at 55 High Street to complain that the doctor's carriage, in turning a corner, had grazed his horse's flank. He died at Oulton Cottage, 26th July 1881.

Blundeston has been immortalized as the birthplace of David
Copperfield. What greater event could have been focused on the
thin round tower of its church that stands up with crenellated
top like a chimney.

> There is nothing half so green that I know anywhere, as the
> grass of that churchyard; nothing half so shady as its trees; noth-
> ing half so quiet as its tombstones. The sheep are feeding there,
> when I kneel up, early in the morning, in my little bed in a closet
> within my mother's room, to look out at it; and I see the red light
> shining on the sun-dial, and think within myself, "Is the sun-dial
> glad, I wonder, that it can tell the time again?"

Here is our pew in the church. What a high-backed pew! With a window near it, out of which our house can be seen, and *is* seen many times during the morning service, by Peggotty, who likes to make herself as sure as she can that it is not being robbed, or not in flames. But though Peggotty's eye wanders, she is much offended ,if mine does, and frowns to me, as I stand upon the seat, that I am to look at the clergyman.

But Dickens was not its only link with literature, for the poet Gray was often a visitor to his friend Norton Nicholls at The Lodge.

Barnby is a small village delighting in a pub known as the Blind Man's Gate, naturally the only one so denominated in the county. The church is of great interest because of extensive wall paintings, now very much faded, and the unique banner-stave closet. This is the only known example with original pierced tracery door. These tall cupboards held the banners carried in the processions.

Gisleham is interesting, steeped in antiquity. There the Hall was enclosed in a double moat and Bloodmore Hill was the site of a battle with the Danes. The church has a round tower. On the easternmost jamb of the north-east nave window is a painting of St. Dorothy, with an angel hovering above. Rushmere church also has a round tower and a banner-stave closet in the south-west corner of the nave. The inn is the 'Three Tuns'.

Flixton (near Bungay) was once the home of the Tasburghs, from whom it passed to the Adairs. The Hall, built by Inigo Jones, was greatly damaged by fire in 1847, but restored. The ruined church was also rebuilt in 1861. Here was an Augustinian nunnery, always hard up. As the park was well stocked with deer, the pub is known as 'The Buck'.

Mutford's little church was once magnificent and shows the beauty that could be lavished on an out-of-the-way sanctuary. It has a round tower with a belfry top and, at its base, a sadly neglected and ruined west or Galilee porch. Suckling points out that these porches were for penitents and also where the dead were sometimes deposited before interment. He deduces the name as being derived from that part of Palestine the most remote from Jerusalem. So these porches are the furthest removed from the sanctuary. There was, and maybe is still, a wall painting of St. Christopher, notable for displaying large sea-shells in the lower part instead of the usual fish.

Barsham, 2 miles from Beccles and 4 from Bungay, is a delightful spot with many ancient memories. The church of Holy Trinity has one of the earliest of the round towers, with a little pricket of a spire. The most interesting feature is the tracery of the east window which extends to the whole of the east end in stone and flint, forming lozenge shapes. The work is sixteenth century, and it is thought the design was suggested by the coat-of-arms of Sir Edward Etchingham, who is buried in the sanctuary. His shield was the east end of the church turned upside down. There is also a stepping block, 'an aid to mounting a horse', that stands at the north-east corner of the tower.

On the floor of the chancel is a brass of a warrior in military costume, wearing an SS collar,* with a lion at his feet. His sword hilt is inscribed 'R.S.' presumably because he held the office of royal seneschal. This has been ascribed to Sir Robert atte Tighe, buried here about 1380.

It is almost incredible to think in this day and age that in June 1970 vandals broke into this church, stole four lengths of oak hacked from the pews and four brass candlesticks.

Barsham church, however, can hardly be considered without its rectory which smiles in its Dutch-like simplicity amid its garden, westward of the round tower. Here, in an old-fashioned and low but cheerful apartment was born on the 27th May 1725 Catherine Suckling, the mother of Nelson; and in the same chamber Maurice, her brother, first saw the light. This was the home of the Reverend Maurice Suckling, Prebendary of Westminster and Rector of Barsham. It was brother Maurice who taught seamanship to the young nephew, who was to become the "merest boy of a Captain I have seen". The central window of the nave south side commemorates the centenary of the Battle of Trafalgar in 1905.

An early and once noble pile, built by the Etchinghams, is to be found in the hinterland behind the church. Now an immense barn

* A collar consisting of a series of Ss and originally a badge of the House of Lancaster.

covered with red pantiles rambles at enormous length what was the banqueting hall of Barsham Hall, where Sir John Suckling, Poet Laureate, housed 100 yeomen at his own expense for King Charles's Scottish wars.

North Cove has a church dedicated to St. Botolph and an excellent example of a Norman south door. The chancel is full of wall paintings that date from the fourteenth century, but have been repainted. On the north wall are some scenes from the Passion, Entry into Jerusalem and the Last Supper. To the east of the north window is the Harrowing of Hell and the Resurrection. On the south wall is the Ascension and a Doom in which coffin-lids figure prominently. The inn is the 'Three Horseshoes'.

> There'll always be an England
>   While there's a country lane,
> Wherever there's a cottage small
>   Beside a field of grain.

So they sang in the second of the world wars, and we are now in such a part of England, where the lanes wander until you come upon a little church such as that at Ellough which stands upon a ridge of what is termed in Suffolk a hill; and, although occupying a rather bleak and naked site, Ellough church looks down upon a rich but narrow valley, in which the rectory and its garden are situated. D. P. Dymond writes that the church may be built on top of a heathen temple. Great Redisham is really small, but Suckling called it the deserted village. The church has a Norman south porch.

It is curious how tastes vary, Suckling describes this south porch as rude Norman architecture so prevalent in the Suffolk village churches. But Munro Cautley says it is a fine example, as the illustration in Suckling's History would suggest.

Ringsfield is a retired village. The rectory and several farmhouses nestle around its church, in a narrow valley fertile, warm and sheltered. The church used to be flooded to the depth of 2 feet or more by a brook that ran nearby. Outside the church on the south chancel wall is a mural tablet with a brass to Nicholas Garneys, c. 1600, and below the east window a tablet commemorating Nicholas Gosling "preacher of God's word", 1663. This

Nicholas was probably responsible for the many texts within, including one on the screen in Latin, which translated means: "A holiness which is mere pretense is double dyed wickedness."

On the north side of the churchyard is one of those marble monumental tombs so dear to the Victorians, which bears this inscription: "H.H. the Princess Caroline Letitia Murat, elder daughter of H.R.H. Prince Murat, grand-daughter of Joachim, King of Naples, and Great Niece of the Emperor, Napoleon I." And remember we are but a stone's throw from Barsham, the birthplace of Nelson's mother.

Shadingfield church is one of the village shrines full of interest. It has a Tudor brick south porch which is worth looking at, and inside an early fifteenth-century octagonal font, standing on a base formed by a Maltese cross. But the prize piece is a treasure in a linen altar cloth, edged with hand-made lace 5 inches wide, the whole cloth measuring 6 feet 6 inches by 3 feet 6 inches. This was in regular use until 1892 and is kept in its original box, $12\frac{1}{2}$ inches square and $2\frac{1}{2}$ inches deep. The box is lined with a patterned paper of the period, and on the inside of the lid is inscribed in script: "This box with a cloath for the Communion table was given to the Parish church of Shadingfield by Elizabeth Cuddon, the wife of William Cuddon gent the xxv day of December, Anno Dmi 1632."

The Cuddons lived in the old Hall, and a "coloured drawing of this demolished specimen of old English dwelling-houses" is to be seen in Suckling's *History*.

Shipmeadow possesses an eighteenth-century House of Industry, one of those horrible visions that haunted rustic old age. A chapel was erected in the grounds from designs by G. E. Street, R.A. This area was in the hands of the Sucklings. He suggests the name should be Sheepmeadow, which is more to the point.

Sotterley is in a smiling oaken country, and the church of St. Margaret is deep in the park. This was the home of the Playters' family and many of their fine brasses are in the church. They came into possession about 1470 when a Red Rose Sotterley lost his land to the Duke of York, afterwards Edward IV. The descendants of Thomas Plafair or Playters retained the manor until 1744, when a John Playters sold it to Miles Barne, who pulled down the old hall and built the present mansion. It was said that Mr. Barne felled sufficient timber to pay the purchase money, and left Sotterley one of the best wooded estates in Suffolk.

In the time of James I, Thomas Playters was High Sheriff for the county. He was said to have been so wealthy that he could ride from Beccles to Dunwich, a distance of 15 miles, upon his own landed property.

On the north wall of the chancel is a large monument to Sir Thomas Playters, knight and baronet, died 1638, and his two wives. By the first he had two sons and two daughters, and by the second, eight sons and ten daughters. These "divers children" are all there kneeling before a fald stool. Hanging in the nave are the King's and Regimental Colours of the Scots Guards presented to Sir Edward Bowater (who married a Barne) after the Peninsular War.

Weston Hall, once a notable house, is now only a fragment of what it was. It was built by John Rede in the latter part of the sixteenth century, when the road ran hard by its walls through an avenue of trees.

One of the most interesting little bits of domestic architecture is to be seen opposite, originally built as a summer or dower house to this same Hall. It is on rising ground southward of the church, built by Thomas Rede in the days of Charles II, whose initials in wrought iron are on the west front. Here is a little gem, with rounded windows and doorways. Dutch influence is very manifest in the design, notably in the brick quoining, the rounding of the gable at its apex, and the filling of the tympanum, as also the dentils under the soffits. Inside are moulded cornices and panelled ceilings. Originally built a floor or two higher, it was supposed to command a view of the sea.

If you go into Weston church, do not fail to see two bench ends in the chancel, one of a seated priest with his book in his lap; the other a post windmill with ladder.

Worlingham Hall as seen today was completed by Robert Sparrow, a local squire about 1800. He was educated at King Edward's Grammar School, Bury St. Edmunds, where he gained a great love of classical literature and collected books enough to fill three rooms of the house. His father had bought the estate in 1755 for £3,850. The house had been built originally by John Felton who died in 1703.

After Sparrow's death in 1822, it passed to his daughter and son-in-law, Lord Gosford. Then to the second Earl, who sold it in 1849. From that time it passed through a number of hands until the present owners, Viscount and Viscountess Colville, acquired it in 1962. Through their own initiative it has been restored to its present fine condition. The staircase is the show-piece of the house, an octagonal structure that is almost unique, with marvellously light and delicate balustrading.

In a hedge in the village once stood a hollow trunk of an immense oak. It afforded shelter for the village cobbler, "who pursued his occupation within its rind; and it is said that the blacksmith once shod a horse within it". The town estate (that was an income from certain charities) was, amongst other purposes, for teaching poor children to read English and for instructing them in the church catechism, "provided that no part of the said rents should be laid out in beer, or any other liquors, at bonfires, or perambulations, or on account of repairing highways".

We now come to the Ilketshalls, known locally as the 'Saints', of which there are four: St. Andrew, St. John, St. Lawrence and St. Margaret. This is Roman Suffolk, because Stone Street goes straight on from Halesworth to Bungay, and the church of St. Lawrence undoubtedly stands on a Roman site.

Suckling makes the interesting statement that among the Saxons mentioned in Domesday as having estates here, "a free woman, whose name is not recorded, appears as an under-tenant of the wealthy Burchard—an early instance of a female Suffolk farmer".

Two of the churches have round towers—those of St. Andrew and St. Margaret. Munro Cautley remarks that a feature of the churchyard of the former is the traditional method of forming the grave mounds. They are built up neatly of turves and bound laterally and longitudinally with withes. A quarter of a mile eastward of St. John's is an entrenchment, consisting of a conical hill, enclosed by a moat.

Mettingham possessed a fourteenth-century castle and college, the latter originally founded at Raveningham in Norfolk, but moved here in 1393. The castle, like Wingfield, a fortified manor house, was built by Sir John de Norwich who obtained a licence from Edward III to castellate his residence in reward for services rendered in the French wars. But it was his wife, Dame Margaret, who built the keep on the west side of the forecourt. It existed as a castle for only forty years. A good deal of the walls remain, the gatehouse being the most interesting feature. The college was inside the enclosure. The church has a round tower and a fine Norman doorway.

This district includes the Elmhams, seven in number if we count Homersfield. Like the Ilketshalls it is a very historic part of the county, especially from the ecclesiastical point of view. The parishes are small and denoted by their churches.

First then comes All Saints, known at one time as All Hallows. This has a very ancient round tower with thick walls. There is, or was, a moated enclosure just south of the churchyard.

South Elmham St. Cross is also known as St. George, and Sancroft from the sandy nature of the soil where the church is situated. Bloomfield, the historian of Norfolk, asserted that the ancestors of the displaced Archbishop Sancroft of Fressingfield derived from this small place. It is also extremely interesting because of the ruin known as the Old Minster, which was thought to have been the cathedral church of the bishops when the see was removed from Dunwich and before it was established at Norwich. It stands in an enclosure said to be Roman, and undoubtedly shows the plan of a very early type of church with apse and western narthex. A rival claim at North Elmham places it there. However, the church of St. George is of great antiquity.

South Elmham St. James has the largest church in the deanery, and is said to stand on the highest ground in the county. From the summit eastward could be seen ships at sea, Poringland, Norwich, and Euston Park. St. James's Park was anciently demesne land of the Bishops of Norwich. A parclose screen in the church has been used to form the wall of a vestry. South Elmham St. Margaret was evidently a seat of bishops, one of whom, Henry de Spencer, the warlike Bishop of Norwich, must have had a castle here similar to those at Mettingham and Wingfield. "Its site which is high and commanding, is encompassed by a broad and deep moat, enclosing about three acres." The chief item of interest in the church is an hour-glass, still in position.

The tale of St. Michael is soon told. The church has a good Norman doorway on the south side. Suckling says: "The minister has no glebe but the churchyard", and that the church is damp, "the edifice standing on a strip of cold wet common land".

At South Elmham St. Peter are the very attractive remains of a moated manor house of the fifteenth century, a sketch of which is shown in Suckling's History. The church is small but well designed, and evoked this very interesting paragraph from the same author:

> In the year 1819, while the writer was visiting this parish, collecting material which form the matter of the present notice, a person of gentlemanly address drove up to St. Peter's Hall, tenanted by the churchwarden, inquiring if the church contained any brass effigies, as he was travelling through the county collecting such records of ancient families, with a view to their cleaning and restoration, promising to return them shortly to their original places. St. Peter's church afforded nothing to add to his collection, having been already stripped by some earlier inconoclast. The writer remembers that the applicant's gig-box was half full of brass effigies, which it is vain to hope ever found again their respective matrices.

There is not a deal to say about Homersfield, which has a bridge over the Waveney, except that according to Suckling the place had so many ale-houses as to give rise to the distich:

> Denton in the dale, and Arbro' in the dirt,—
> And if you go to Homersfield your purse will get the squirt.

However, the Waveney here has been stocked with brown trout recently by the Suffolk and Norfolk River Board.

Rumburgh is worth a visit. A small priory or cell to St. Benet's, Hulme and later to St. Mary's, York, was to be found here. It was dissolved by Wolsey for the endowment of his college at Ipswich. The truncated west tower of the church with its weather-boarded top presents an interesting appearance. Within is a once magnificent screen, the tracery of the upper panels being very rich. There is not much to say about Spexhall except that its once ruined and ivy-covered round tower was rebuilt in recent years. Sir Edward Kerrison was lord of the manor in Victorian times and George Kerrison the parish clerk. Stoven is tucked away from the busy world, and the church has a fine Norman doorway. When I was there a woodman made hurdles and wooden implements. He also made his own cider by the pailful. It lacked nothing in strength. Brampton is on the once busy line to Lowestoft. At the Hall lived the Leman family, one of whom founded the Free School in Beccles, endowed in 1631.

Munro Cautley has a lot to say about the church at Westhall. To him it presented the most interesting illustration of the growth of a parish church. It has some elaborate Norman work at the end of the south aisle, which was originally the nave. Early in the fourteenth century the building was enlarged by an extension on the north side, the old wall being pierced with arcades. The fine chancel was built about 1370. The base of the rood screen remains, with some very interesting figures in the panels, one of which shows Christ transfigured with a gold face. Also, here is one of the Seven Sacrament fonts, which is remarkable in showing more of the original colouring than any other. In Penance the devil is seen making his exit on the right. Horse trappings found in a field link the parish with the Iron Age, while the roof of the church provided a hiding place for smuggled goods, although it is some distance from the scene of landing. Here was the residence of Edmund Bohun, political writer and antiquarian at the time of James II, William III, and Queen Anne.

Frostenden holds a good deal of interest because at the time of the Domesday it was returned as a seaport for shipping and had a salina or salt-works, the working of which had been abandoned when the Survey was made up. Suckling says the *portus maris* must have been situated somewhere in the little valley now called Frostenden Bottom. He goes on to say how many of the unimportant rivulets that flow to the sea were navigable for the small craft of early commerce, or ancient predatory warfare for that matter.

The church has a notable round tower, which illustrates once again their attachment to water courses. It shows, too, how all kinds of material were used in construction, as one or two querns can be traced in the rubble. The little porch adjoining has a sundial over the entrance, with the inscription: *"Vigilate et Orate"*.

Sotherton St. Andrew was rebuilt in 1854, but it has a splendid example of a font cover. This is pyramidal in shape, dating from the seventeenth century and about 6 feet high. It covers a traditional East Anglian font.

However small the village, it holds something of historic interest; this is usually to be found in the church. Such is the case with South Cove, tucked away in a by-road not far from Southwold. How many bells once hung in its belfry to spill their typical English music on that still air is not known, but is reflected in the inn of the 'Five Bells'.

It is only a tiny church but there is so much to it, with Norman doors north and south. The north doorway was fitted in the fifteenth century with a panelled door of great beauty. This has traceried and crocketted heads to the panels and is still in place. But the church's pride and joy is the rare survival of the original door to the rood loft stairs, painted with a figure of St. Michael. One of the fifteenth-century bells has a Latin inscription which means: "May Peter lead us to the joys of eternal life."

Benacre cannot be missed with its lovely park of 230 acres that skirts the A12 as it draws near to Lowestoft. This is the home of Sir Robert and Lady Gooch. His name has been long associated with splendid farming, and the famous Benacre Flock of Suffolk Sheep was only dispersed in 1968. A Mr. Carhew built the Hall and after his death it was sold to Thomas Gooch for £15,800 in 1743. The Gooch family evidently came from Mettingham, where a Thomas Gooch was landowner in the early part of the sixteenth century.

It was a Sir Thomas Gooch who was the first person to suggest

to the Government the plan of raising provincial corps of yeomanry cavalry throughout the kingdom. His proposal was made in
December 1729 and soon after adopted generally in Great Britain
and Ireland. Sir Thomas bore the rank of First Lieutenant under
Lord Rous in the first troop of the Suffolk yeomanry to be organ-
ized in the county.

In 1876 a hoard of Roman coins was dug up in the park, and a
clump of trees near the road is called 'Money Tree Clump'. Benacre Broad, a lovely sheet of fresh water, is well stocked with jack,
tench, roach and other fish. The village is ideally situated, winding
its way towards the sea, but the church rebuilt in 1769 contains
nothing of great interest.

Wrentham has a fine church, with effigies in brass of a lady
Ele Bowet, 1400, and another in armour of Humphreys Brewster,
1593; with one or two iron grave memorials in the churchyard,
evidence of a local ironworks. It also has a good example of an
honest-to-goodness Congregational Chapel. In the minister's
house was born J. Ewing Richie, who left his memoirs behind. As
a little boy he decided to run away from home, and got as far as
Yoxford. There he was intercepted by Mr. Bird, the local poet, who
kept a shop. That fine old chapel still remains, with stabling for
the gigs of the farmers who formed a large part of the congregation. Evidence of the 'Guche' family, since it is their village, is
seen in buildings that line the way.

In the time of the threatened invasion by Napoleon, the tower
of the church was used as a signal station, and a wooden signal
house for the accommodation of the sentinels was erected in the
churchyard.

Wangford comes next, a peaceful little village on the A12,
where the church has been much restored. This is really the home
of the Rous family, as Henham, where once the Hall stood, is a
hamlet of this parish. Henham contains within its quiet fields
some ancient earthworks known as Henham Moat Yards. An oak
in Henham Park still exists where, it is said, a Royalist Rous hid
himself, exemplifying his Royal master.

Reydon is the home of a splendid public school for girls, that
of St. Felix with its motto—*Felix Quia Fortis*. Nearby, hard to

find, is Wolsey Bridge, over which, it is said, the young cardinal-to-be drove the cattle towards his father's slaughterhouses.

Reydon Hall was the home of the Stricklands, built 1603. Agnes, co-authoress with her sister Elizabeth of the *Queens of England*, could be met with in Southwold, driving in her gig, wearing her Georgian gold rings on the outside of her gloved fingers. They were clever literary daughters of Thomas Strickland. Another sister, Catherine, married Thomas Traill, a half-pay officer of the Royal Scots Fusiliers, and emigrated with him to the backwoods of Canada, where she became known as the 'Botanist of the Backwoods'. She grew to be a venerated figure, sought out as one of the most interesting women in the country. The first gathering of her botanical notes appeared in 1868, a landmark in the history of Canadian botany, under the title of *Canadian Wild Flowers*, published in Montreal. The Indians gave her a name of their own, 'Red Cloud of the Dawn', because of her English (Suffolk) complexion.

Suckling tells us that Holton signifies the village of the wood. It was probably part of the vast forest which stretched around Halesworth and its vicinity, mentioned in Domesday. It possesses two or three features, a crinkle-crankle wall, an early round tower to the church, with a Norman south doorway. And what is more, and decidedly a welcome sight, a post mill that has been restored by youthful enthusiasts.

Blyford, as its name implies, has a ford over the Blyth. The church is old, with interesting Norman doorways both south and north, and perhaps the best Holy Table in the county, with fine bulbous carved legs.

In the churchyard, wrought by a mason artist in stone but with all the charm of a woodcut, is a memorial to a servant in husbandry, who died at the early age of 21. He was a ploughman and is depicted with a couple of Suffolk Punches, an old wooden plough with whipple-trees and is himself wearing a smock, buskins and a characteristic hat. A statuette of Venus was found near Blyford Bridge.

There is much to say about Blythburgh, for this is indeed historic ground, one might say prehistoric. Many churches were built in strong defensive positions, frequently difficult of access from the village and probably erected on a site utilized by prehistoric man. Blythburgh church is one of these and may account for its preservation when the village was destroyed by a succession of fires. At nearby Bulcamp, Anna, king of East Anglia, with his capital at Dunwich, fought the old heathen Penda in 654. He was killed after a reign of nineteen years and with him fell his son Jurmin. Along Anna's Lane, tree-lined, sweetened with briar and honeysuckle, it is said, they carried the body of their dead king to rest awhile in an earlier church, in all probability made of wood.

Jurmin also rested in the church, but as M. R. James reminds us: "In the eleventh century the body was appropriated, no doubt to the disgust of the Blythburgh people, by the masterful convent of Bury, and there, at or near the Chapel of the Virgin in the central eastern apse of the Abbey church (as I think) a handsome silver shrine contained it until the Dissolution. The shrine figured in the great processions: the commemorations were on February 23 and May 31."

Blythburgh, Holy Trinity, has probably been the subject of more pictures in the Royal Academy than any other Suffolk church. This noble building within and without rises magic-like out of the marshes, and must have been the finest in the county when in its glory. It is glorious now but can be only a shadow of what it once was, for the despoiler's hand has been heavy, and not long ago was almost in ruins. The light from its many windows, for it is a splendid example of Perpendicular work, rebuilt about 1450, now shines coldly on its emptiness. But there are evidences and memories that linger, filling it again with the pageantry that moved along its aisles.

Inside, the angel roof (such roofs are only to be found in this part of the county) was once full of coats-of-arms and is supported by ten great tie-beams. The wing feathers are painted red, blue, white and green, while the feathers of the body match. These figures have been well peppered with shot by Dowsing's men. Some of the wings were replaced in 1954. The base of the screen now appears to form fronts for the choir stalls, and show a fine array of well-cut canopied figures of the Fathers of the Church.

The most remarkable feature is the early examples of bench-ends, denoting the Seven Deadly Sins and the Seasons. Unfortunately these have been sadly mutilated but they still tell the story of sins that befell our ancestors as those that beset us today. The Seasons, so well observed by those early worshippers, told of life's round that passed in those local fields.

The lectern is worthy of notice, particularly as a robin took the liberty of building a nest within its quatrefoiled interior; not only so but it brought off a brood. There is also an early and splendid example of a poor box, a receptacle employed in every church before the establishment of Poor Laws, to collect alms of the charitable. A small school was once held in the Clopton chantry. Inkwells were cut in the book rests, and one boy spent his time leaving a memorial by cutting his name in the wood—"Dirck Lowerson van Stockholm, Anno N 1665 AG 12". He must have been a son of one of the Flemish weavers or of a Dutchman who came here on dyking work.

There is also what was once a good example of a Seven Sacrament Font. It was badly damaged by the fall of the spire in 1577. Round the steps is an inscription to John and Katherine Masin, who also erected the porch. Neither should we miss the Jack o' the Clock, with the inscription:

As the hours pass away,
So doth the life of man decay. 1682.

There are not many of these about but there is another at Southwold.

Outside, the beauty of the building with its clerestory and pinnacles is an eternal monument to those old masons. Among the figures is Christ and the Virgin, while others are demoniac or symbolic; but note the bear with a chain round its neck, reminiscent of those that perambulated the countryside for the amusement of the populace. There is a fine south porch with groined roof supporting an upper chamber, and nearby a holy water stoup of unusual proportions, and perhaps the best specimen. The reason for its preservation is said to have been that it was found built into the wall the other way round, hidden by careful hands against the despoiler. Under the east window is a line of capital letters, crowned, and executed in flush-work. No one knows their import but guesses have been made. Blythburgh was the last church visited by William Morris in his Society for the Preservation of Ancient Buildings campaign, just before he died.

The remains of the Augustinian Priory, north-east of the church, are negligible, but two thatched houses, built out of these ruins, retain the memory. One house was restored by Ernest Crofts, R.A., and the other by John Seymour Lucas, R.A.

Having said so much about the church we must visit the 'White Hart', one of Suffolk's fine old inns. It has some good woodwork within, but it may have been the court house when Blythburgh was of great importance from a shipping and industrial point of view. Its Dutch-like gable end stood firm amid the fires of 1667 and 1696, when the centre of the old merchant town went up in flames.

Blythburgh, as one might suppose, has a ghost—Black Toby, who walks the Common at certain times. He was a coloured drummer attached to Sir Robert Rich's regiment, stationed here, and was hanged for the murder of Anne Blakemore in 1750.

Just one thing more—when an old cottage known as the Alms-houses was destroyed by fire, it was occupied by an old man who greatest treasure was a china toilet set. A neighbour anxious to rescue such a possession threw it out of the window.

We will leave Blythburgh to the beauty of its estuarine waters, the marshes with their fringe of poplars, the heronry and the wistful green of its dykes and river, and go to Thorington, which is tucked away westward of the A12. The one great object of interest is the very unusual round tower to the church. A curious form of arched arcading has been worked into the lower course, while Norman work is seen in the upper windows. Set amid trees, on rising ground that gently falls away to the marsh lands of the river, it is well worth a visit.

Walpole has the oldest chapel in East Anglia, established 1646, the second oldest in the country. Although 300 years old it is the same inside as when first opened for worship. Amidships, is a ship's mast around which the whole fabric hangs; it is said to have

The moated Hall at Helmingham

High Street, Debenham

Framlingham Castle

The Crinkle-Crankle Wall at Bramfield

Dunwich beach looking towards Southwold

Burgh Castle

The gateway to Greyfriars Monastery, Dunwich

come from Yarmouth. With the overhanging galleries, one has the impression of being in the hold of a ship although not now on the seas of controversy. There is an endowment of land and houses, one of the latter being for the minister.

Wenhaston church is of considerable antiquity, but its great-treasure is the sixteenth-century 'Doom', discovered almost miraculously in 1892, when restoration work was in progress. This wonderful painting of the Last Judgement formed a wooden tympanic filling to the chancel arch, that was taken down and thrown outside. Very heavy rain in the night washed off some of the plaster and exposed the figures. These boards were further cleansed and put together under the direction of a very intelligent vicar, the Reverend J. B. Clare. It is unique as having been painted around the Holy Rood, which was attached to it in the centre, and its preservation was due to the whitewash covering. It has been conjectured that it was the work of a monk of Blythburgh, to which the advowson belonged. A very early school was started in Wenhaston in 1562, William Pepyn leaving land to the town for its support.

Bramfield, now west of the A12, was an important village at the time of the Domesday survey. It was on the direct road from London to Bungay, for an ancient oak, the remains of which are still visible in the park of Bramfield Hall, was a Waymark, commemorated in the lines describing Bigod's flight from the King.

> When the Bailey had ridden to Bramfield Oak,
> Sir Hugh was at Ilketshall Bower;
> When the Bailey had ridden to Halesworth Cross,
> He was singing in Bungay Tower—
> "Now that I am in my castle of Bungay,
> Upon the river of Waveney,
> I will ne care for the King of Cockney."

This happened about 1174, so the fragment is near 1,000 years old. But further proof of Bramfield's antiquity is to be found opposite, in earthworks of an oval moated enclosure. Another remarkable fact was that the poll-tax, levied in the reign of Richard II, continued to be collected by the parson, 4d. per person, in this parish until the year 1805. It was stopped through the opposition of a Mr. Page.

The thatched church has a detached round tower, the only one of the type, with walls 5 feet thick. It contains five bells, three being medieval. But the glory of this village church is its lovely screen, the finest in Suffolk. It is in excellent preservation and carved in delicate tracery, painted and gilded. The canopy is finely groined, interspersed with golden angels, while a graceful crock-etted arch forms the portal. The shafts are covered in gesso work, coloured blue and red in diaper designs in rich profusion. The panels in the lower portion have paintings of SS. Mark, Matthew, Luke, John and the Magdalene, carried out in heraldic colours.

On the north wall of the chancel is the touchingly wrought effigy of Mrs. Arthur Coke by Nicholas Stone. She died in child-birth, and here she lies with her babe, portrayed in all the pathos of such an end. Her husband in armour kneels in a niche above her.

Opposite the church, flanking the road and running round three sides of the garden of the Hall, is the best example of a crinkle-crankle wall. Built one brick thick and curved for strength, it pro-vides an artistic enclosure for an old garden, and a shelter for wall-fruit and flowers.

Darsham, with its rose-hung station on the old Great Eastern Railway, was to me as the gate of heaven when I used to come with my mother to visit my grandparents. It was all so different from our London suburban home, for here the railway ran over the road and great gates opened and closed to let the old blue engines pass. Then, just outside in the sweet-smelling air, grand-father would be waiting with his pony cart to take us to his farm-yard home.

Yoxford, nearby, is often described as the 'Garden of Suffolk'. So it is in many ways, but so are many other Suffolk villages. Cockfield Hall, the home of the Blois family, has Tudor memories in its old red bricks, although it has been much altered. The Hall proper evidently had a hammer-beam roof with good carving, and there was some nice plaster work within, but a good deal of re-building has been carried out so that little of the original house remains. Lady Katherine Grey, the exquisitely pretty sister of Jane, was finally incarcerated here for marrying, without permission, the Earl of Hertford. She came in October 1567 and died of tuberculosis at the age of 28 on the 22nd of the following January. Buried in the village church for a time, her coffin was later taken to Salisbury Cathedral, where she lies with her husband under a magnificent memorial. A room in the Hall is still known as her chamber. Reyce, writing in 1619, says, "I have been told by aged people in Yoxford that, after her death, a little dog she had would never eat any more meat, and lay and died upon her grave." One of the treasures of the Hall is her travelling trunk, covered with cordovan leather and iron bound.

John of Norwich first held Cockfield Hall, from whom it passed to John Hopton, whose grandson, Sir Owen, sold it to Robert Brooke, Alderman of London. His grand-daughter married Sir William Blois of Grundisburgh, to which family it passed. The outbuildings comprise a north wing and a gatehouse, the latter built sideways to the Hall, which dates from the first half of the sixteenth century. This gatehouse is as good a gem of English brickwork as any to be found in the county. It is built of old English pattern small bricks, laid in English bond; that is courses of headers, alternating with those of stretchers, with wide joints. The gables are crow-stepped, resting on kneelers, and surmounted by excellent examples of moulded brick chimneys. The stabling also is an old building, while the yard has two brick gateways, one new and the other old, with a dove-cote, also modern, set within. These outbuildings have been sadly damaged by enemy action. The little river Yox, later to turn to the Min, runs pleasantly through the parklands, as once it provided a moat to the house.

Which brings us to the village itself. Certainly it is pretty and picturesque, and was more so before the famous 'Three Tuns' was burnt down and its bowling green lost. It is also surrounded by nice estates such as Grove Park and The Rookery. As you walk down the village you pass an ancient house, once an inn known as the 'Maid's Head', and reputed to have belonged to Cardinal Wolsey's uncle. The church, besides some good brasses, has a spire, an unusual but picturesque feature, and a fine peal of bells. Note also the Tudoresque camouflage to the side of the shop that abuts on to the terrace to the Hall.

At Sibton there are some ruins of the only Cistercian House in Suffolk, reminder of the ancient gardeners with their green fingers. The very much restored church, set on a hill, has a rebus on its name in the roof.

Peasenhall village is in a valley with houses on both sides of a little stream that trickles along in peaceful serenity. Here were the extensive agricultural iron works of Smyth and Sons, the original inventors of the Suffolk Seed Drill. Just recently Blyth Rural Council offered for sale some cottages which, on examination of the deeds, turned out to be an old Wool Hall. The house, built about 1455 by one of the abbots of Sibton, was also known as the New Inn and may have been used as a hostelry to house the overflow of guests from the hospice of the abbey.

Peasenhall came into wide prominence in June 1902, when Rose Harsent, a young woman of 22, a maid at Providence House, was found murdered. William Gardiner, a local man employed at Smyth's, was accused, but after a second trial acquitted.

We will now pass the eastern side of the hundred and go to Westleton which is a very large village. The church was once under the abbots of Sibton. This parish is remarkable for the amount of folk-lore within its borders. For example, a stone near the priest's door is said never to be overgrown with grass. For many generations Westleton boys and girls, even young men and women, took part in running round the church seven or three times, using this stone as a base. The custom was to place a hand-kerchief or straw in the grating in the wall above the stone, then run eastwards, northwards and back to the stone via the west end, never looking at the grating until the end. On the completion of the run, the article placed was said to disappear, or you heard the devil clanking his chains below the grating.

Ghosts were very active here: there was one that haunted the Red Stile at the extremity of the village near the Red Farm. Then, at some cottages that skirted the churchyard wall, the occupants at night could often hear their tea-cups and china being moved about by the Little Folk who used their kitchen. It was also well known that if you left your room clean and tidy for them they would leave a bright new coin in the bowl in payment. In an 1851 list of inhabitants there were two nurses, one of which bore the useful name of Aholibamah Cogman.

Middleton-cum-Fordley was the home of my grandparents, and to reach it from Westleton in the old days one had to cross over a splash. I have written about it so often that I must not dilate upon it now. It is a largely unspoiled village, probably because of its position, and is grouped in two sections, one, known as the Street, around the village green, the other towards Yoxford, called the Moor. At one time there were two churches in the one churchyard. The present church of Holy Trinity has a tall, lead-covered spire once surmounted by a golden cockerel. A few years ago the church was almost destroyed by fire when the thatched roof caught alight during repairs to the spire. Near the Norman south door is a gravestone inscribed: "In Memory of Charles Godward of Her Majesty's 16th Lancers, who distinguished himself in the battles of Mahrajpoor, Ruddawal, Aliwal and Sobraon. He died at the age of 52 years, 1871."

Here was one of those long tenures in the post office, when a family held it for ninety-seven years, ending the term in 1946. Joseph Broom anticipated events by having a box placed in his little shop for mail. A postman named Bob Marshlain used to arrive on horseback, heralding his approach by blowing a horn. Broom was appointed in 1849 and was succeeded by his daughter who married a Barham.

Middleton Moor, once a camping ground for gipsies and a place where prize fights took place, as well as open-air baptisms, also has a particularly fine example of a Tudor brick gable-end to a farm-house. Inside is a wonderful specimen of local pargeting in an overmantel to an upstairs room, once used for lumber. Fordley Hall is another fine old house, south of the moor.

Theberton comes next with another round tower. The church has an extremely fine Norman north doorway, now forming the entrance to a vestry. Charles Montagu Doughty (1843–1926) was born at the Hall. Out of two years' travel and hardship in Arabia in 1875–77, slowly grew his great book, *Arabia Deserta*. This prose classic was published in 1888. Down by the marshes, not far from the sea, is a lonely little pub called the 'Eel's Foot'. Not only the inn but the church were known to smugglers.

Knodishall, a friendly village, was known miles around for its Cold Fair held on 11th December. Aldringham is a straggling village with a pub, 'The Parrot and Punchbowl'—evidently reminiscent of "Home is the sailor, home from the sea". A post mill here was removed to nearby Thorpeness to join the House in the Clouds that masks a water tower. A barrow exists on the green. Kelsale and Carlton complete the list of the Blything Hundred. Although taken together they are really separate parishes. Kelsale church has been much rebuilt but it has a peal of eight bells, after which the pub is named. There is a ancient Guildhall that has now become the first East Suffolk Teachers' Centre. Carlton church, tucked away in the park, has a notable Holy Table.

And so to Debenham, with its street of overhanging timbered houses and old-world flavour. Here is the source of the Deben, and here is Crow's Hall. This was built about 1508, so named from one Crowe, a gentleman according to an ancient chronicler; but of its early owners little seems to be known. It came into prominence when the home of the Carolean knight, Sir Charles Framlingham, and his son-in-law, Sir Charles Bassingbourne Gawdy. Surrounded by a moat 9 feet deep, it is the perfect and unaltered example of an ancestral home of red brick, set amid flowers that grow, not merely about its grass-covered walks, but out of the crannies of the mossy walls—pennywort, stonecrop, crane's-bill, yellow wallflowers and the houseleek. Timelessness is expressed in beauty within and without.

This haunt of ancient peace, tucked away at the end of a long avenue of old oaks, has a correspondingly aged barn, or line of outbuildings known as the 'Barracks', suggestive of the Cavalier's retainers. These are decorated with moulded brick-arched mullioned windows to match the Hall. Rumour had it that another line of buildings stood adjacent, but have disappeared because of Cromwell's cannons.

The church of St. Mary has another of those western or Galilee porches, and a peal of eight bells, with a pub to match. Also between here and Brice's Farm is a boulder stone that is said to groan at midnight.

Framsden has the distinction of being centrally situated between Ipswich, Woodbridge and Stowmarket, eleven miles from each. Here again is a peal of eight bells. The church of St. Mary has an exceptionally fine and unusual Stuart Holy Table, dated 1628. But Framsden has something more in the shape of a Post-mill which has been completely restored by a devoted band of enthusiasts. An old apple tree provided teeth for the cog wheels that drive the stones; while hornbeam was used for teeth for the brake wheel— this was from a tree blown down in Shrubland Park a few years ago. It is hoped to complete the work by 1972, and thus replace a bit of Suffolk scenery that has been turning for nearly 200 years.

Pettaugh has a very small church dedicated to St. Catherine. There is a small brass probably to one of the Fastolfe family, a civilian in gown and wife in pedimental head-dress described by Farrar as "local and peculiar". Recently a palimpsest brass was found. A tablet on the west wall records a gift to the parish, 8th March 1842, of a cottage, garden and 2 acres of land, the rent of which to go to sexton's wages, church repairs and parish expenses. The Post-mill ceased to work at the start of the Second World War.

3

The Coastal Villages

We are as near to heaven by sea as by land.

THE coastal villages naturally form a very interesting and distinct collection of parishes, particularly as this coast has been so subject to erosion, as it was also the victim of depredations by early invaders. However, in all fairness, we must realize that it was through our coastal settlements that enlightening influences came and made the South Folk what they are, even distinct from their neighbours, the North Folk. We might begin the story with Corton and the couplet:

> When you come to Corton,
> The way begin to shorten.

This was a term used by the fishermen in the days of sail, beating homewards, because Corton church stands high and can be seen miles to seaward. Suckling tells us that once upon a time Corton stood inland, with the village of Newton between it and the sea. Now the latter has entirely disappeared and possibly become the treacherous Corton Sands. The church is a ruin, save for the chancel, and its chief treasure is a floriated fourteenth-century stone gable cross, which shows the Crucifixion one side and the Virgin and Child on the other.

Pakefield had a very interesting church in that it was a double one, in which were two naves and two altars, the latter approached by steps crossing the full width of the naves. Each half of the church was separately dedicated, one to All Saints, the other to

St. Margaret. They were really two churches placed side by side, divided by a wall and served two parishes. On the 30th June 1743 the two livings were consolidated into one.

Today the fishermen's church perched on the cliff proudly announces the fact that, having been destroyed by enemy action on 14th April 1941, it was rebuilt in June 1950, and the original covering of thatch adhered to. This was really remarkable considering the decline in numbers of thatched churches, even in the two counties which might be described as the home of thatch. This typical Suffolk church stands as a beautiful memorial (with the village stocks and manacles), a witness to the indestructibility of the Faith, not only of those who go down to the sea in ships, but of those who sow to reap.

Coast erosion has been heavy here. In the Ship Inn, now gone, was a rough painting showing some shipwrecked men being hauled ashore by Peek, a well-known lugger skipper, and under it these lines:

> She strikes the sand, she parts the deck,
> The crew now float upon the wreck,
> But safe from harm God guards the strand
> And keeps his Roaring Boys at hand.

Next to this was a painting of a black pyramidal tombstone inscribed:

> To the Memory of Robert Peek and his Crew,
> Drowned October 30th, 1836. Memento mori.

Pakefield was the home of the Roaring Boys about whom a long ballad grew up, sung in the sheds of the old Beach Companies in chorus, especially the refrain:

> The Roaring Boys of Pakefield,
> O, Nobly do they thrive!
> They had but one poor parson,
> And they buried him alive.

One version of the tale runs that the parson had been to Lowestoft and imbibed too freely. He was walking home along the sand when he came over giddy and fell near the water's edge. The incoming tide revived him sufficiently to crawl up the shore where he fell asleep. Later, two of his parishioners saw a sodden bundle lying there, went to investigate, and were horrified to discover it was their own parson. They placed the body in a hollow and went home to the sleeping village to blaze the news. They then proceeded to collect an undertaker, constable, lanterns, and such-like gear, and returned to bring home the corpse. Their astonishment was great when they found the old man sitting up in the hole, spluttering and using rather bad language.

But we must not forget it was a saintly vicar, the Reverend Francis Cunningham, who was called upon to conduct the burial service over a 'dead seaman' at eight o'clock in the morning. He discovered later he had performed the last rites over a load of valuable lace.

Kessingland has been subject to much coast erosion. Suckling tells us that "a piece of ground known as Sea Row was swept away. . . . Two wells were then standing, which rose like tunnels in the sand". Of the church, the original fifteenth-century tower backed by trees is very fine; 95 feet high, it forms a notable sea-mark. The fourteenth-century font is one of the finest in the county. St. Edmund figures in one of the niches, holding the peak of his beard in his right hand.

One other laconic memory: "Edward Carleton, Vicar, did promise several times to give five pounds towards the rebuilding of Kessingland church, and gave not a penny." He must have been like King John when he went to Bury Abbey. He offered not a sou but borrowed something of the abbot.

Covehithe church of St. Andrew is a picturesque but noble ruin. It was one of the finest churches in the county, rivalling Blythburgh for magnificence and proportion.

Walberswick, the town by the wood, means many things to many people. To some, seamanship, shipwrecks, fishing and a life of hazard; of piracy and smuggling. And yet to others, boat building and high farming, with large flocks of sheep. It was known in local parlance as 'Walserwig', with the uncomplimentary adage: "He's a Walserwig whisperer-Yow ma' har' him ova t' Sowle." This was for a loud-mouthed person. Then the port in common with its neighbours bore the description:

To Dunswich, Sowle and Walserwick,
We pass in at a lousy crick.

What a curious, almost incoherent picture it presents: here a green, there old sheds once used to kipper herrings; and old houses that look like children's playthings, including shacks on stilts, the figure-head of a ship, the nameboard of some old wreck, such as the *Concord*, that might have been to New England and back. And there by the Hard, where the old chain ferry has ceased to cough, is a flock of the cleanest geese you could meet on any village green. However, they will warn you off their native and lovely reach, calling to mind that local version sung by Walberswick children of yester year:

> Candlemas Day,
> Hussy goose lay;
> At Valentine
> Your goose and mine.

Like all medieval townships, built largely of wood, Walberswick has been devastated by fire. First in the sixteenth century and again in 1633 and 1683, when apparently it was set on fire, and again in 1749. Flooding by extremely high tides has also been a great danger, occurring at intervals during the years, one particularly bad occasion being in 1898. But surely the worst flood of all came on that awful night of 31st January 1953 at about 10 p.m. After an almost idyllic spring-like day on the Thursday, a north-west gale sprang up, causing winds of fearful velocity on the Saturday night, this joined an exceptionally high tide in a fearful alliance.

A petition of the inhabitants in 1652 speaks of "our poor town, now one of the poorest towns in England, not being able to repair our church or Meeting Place, which at first was reared up by the Inhabitants at their only cost and charge, and the many poor widows and fatherless and motherless children and at present not above one man living in the town that has £5, per year of his own".

But the tale of ships and seamanship is as old as Walberswick; it runs as a weft to its warp, of sons that never came home again, epitomized in that ill-fated smack, *The Clipper*, which disappeared with all hands in a calm North Sea one September day in 1883. Four widows were left in a population of only 130 souls; and the little dingy "with only about two inches of water in her".

The sailor was always surrounded by an aura of superstition. For example, when *The Clipper* was lost, the grandmother of two brothers on board saw them going up towards their house the very night they were lost. Again, it was an omen of evil to meet a female on the way to join a boat. And "A Friday's sail, Always fail". Their womenfolk said—"Never wash on the day your man go away or you wash him away"! And "Don't let a loaf of bread lie on its side, or a boat will go over".

But what would you say, or think, of a place where they called a windlass a 'crab'? And when fishing was bad they would take to 'bousing', which was an alias for fishing for anchors.

A silent, pathetic and almost obliterated memorial of sea-faring life is to be found in the churchyard on the south-west side. It is a headstone on which is cut an eighteenth-century cutter-rigged vessel, above this inscription: "In memory of Elizabeth, the loving wife of Thomas Archer, who departed this life, March 20, 1781, aged 37 years." A Thomas Archer was master of the *Dunwich* of 60 tons, built at Ipswich in 1778, and sold to Lynn in 1803.

No account of Walberswick would be complete without mention of the famous Southwold Railway, opened on 24th September 1879. The entire personnel could be counted on the fingers of two hands. The crossing of the river here was by a swing bridge and, for safety, lest the gate should be opened unawares, a key was handed to the driver at Southwold, left by him at Blythburgh and picked up again on the return journey. The last train ran in 1929 and the rolling stock went for scrap in the Second World War. The distance covered was a little over 9 miles, with stations at Wenhaston, Blythburgh and Walberswick. Walter Doy, one of the platelayers, was prosecuted in 1884 for setting snares and taking hares *en route*.

Another and kindred institution was the old Pontoon Chain Ferry. For many years George Todd pulled the string that caused the whistle to shriek, and drove the load into the tide. It was run on chains from bank to bank, to ramps constructed for the purpose; and before the donkey engine was installed it appears to have been operated by hand. It had a nasty habit of sinking on occasions.

Some of the old houses remain and are incorporated in the new Walberswick, but much is new and of a modern character. One timber-framed house of great character is not a native at all. It was uprooted bodily from Lavenham and set down here. One has to be thankful it didn't go to America.

To Walberswick belongs the distinction of possessing the first Women's Institute for East Suffolk. Its inception was at a meeting held on 9th September 1918. All this can be seen on the first page, illuminated, of the minute book.

The magnificent tower of the church of St. Andrew's is 95 feet high, of four stages, constituting a superb landmark, not only for the surrounding countryside, but for those early adventurers at sea. The contract for its erection has survived and is an interesting example of its kind.

The bird life of Walberswick is very considerable epitomized in the eighteenth-century brick-towered Pumping Mill, used long enough in local parlance for 'grinding water'. With its boat-shaped cap and cloth sails it gave point and character to the marshes in which so many watchers found their quarry. These marshes are chiefly notable for passage waders in spring and autumn, when the birds congregate. The Bittern breeds here and its peculiar boom, akin to a ship's siren, can be heard in the spring. An occasional avocet can sometimes be seen, while garganey, sandwich terns and Montagu's harriers are summer visitors. In the autumn, greenshanks, knots, ruffs, godwits and green sandpipers are visitors, and many terns, sometimes in flocks. In the winter hen harriers, hooded crows, waxwings, twites, merlins are frequently seen. Rarities that have been noted include American pectoral sandpiper and shore larks. Numerous species breed in the district, notably stone curlews, whinchats, red-backed shrikes, gadwall, marsh harriers and bearded tits. The latter are really beautiful little birds, with a metallic note. They were known as reed pheasants, and may be seen running up the reeds like a mouse, or flying with a dipping motion.

Walberswick has been for long the peculiar patrimony of artists, as it shows a wonderful gradation of colour and play of light and shade, ripple of wind and glimpses of sunshine on sea and river. Peter de Wint (1784–1849) painted a water-colour of the ruined church, with cows in the churchyard. This is now at Christchurch Mansions, Ipswich. Both the Seymour Lucases, R.A., painted here, and others almost too numerous to mention. J. Doman Turner, an amateur artist who had studied under Sickert, conceived the idea of creating a Walberswick Scroll. This is a pictorial record of all the houses in the village, set out on a continuous sheet, some 123 feet long. It was executed in the summer of 1931–2, and is now in the Southwold Museum.

The name of Phillip Wilson Steer (1860–1942) stands easily first amongst the local memories. It was here that, according to MacColl, this portrayer of atmosphere and of light, an impressionist, painted his most personal pictures, in which he was really himself and in which "the people are flaunting themselves like flags". Robin Ironside also writes of him: ". . . in the gentle inrush of the waves of his Ermine Sea, or the airy langours that seem to flutter off the waters at evening beyond the pierhead at Walberswick, the painter has gathered up all the entranced sensations of youthful visits to the seaside".

There were living models to be found here, shellbacks and young fishermen with the bearing of gods. Not forgetting Dolly Brown, daughter of a fisherman, Jonah Brown. She was one of four sons and four daughters all of whom seem to have been painted at some time or another. She figures in some of Steer's pictures, who later shared her with Edward Poynter.

It is not a long way to Dunwich, which we can reach by walking along the beach or going round by the road, and it is no exaggeration to say that this hamlet is the most interesting, as it is the most historic in the whole of East Anglia. For here, under the tide, lies the capital city of the old kingdom. If, at early morning or at evening when the shadows lengthen, you stand silently on the cliffs you will experience a peculiar strangeness that this is no ordinary place. And your feelings will be justified, because beneath your feet is indeed antiquity, "where Man hath been".

Dunwich has been spoken of as a 'dead city', but I venture to think it is anything but that. For Dunwich men and women live again, not only in artefacts and recorded echoes but in the very atmosphere. Even the old fishermen thought themselves immortal, and that when they died they were turned into gulls.

All classes of society lived and enjoyed the liberty and freedom of this old city. That most exclusive club, the Knights' Templars, had a preceptory here, well furnished and supplied with mazers and gold and silver cups. At the other extreme was the haven for lepers. True, it was without the gate, but nevertheless it was here —and wealthy at that. Illness, loathsome and contagious, demanded sympathy and care, particularly as it was a common heritage. An escutcheon of many quarterings was no safeguard against plague, neither would complete armour act as a shield from such an enemy.

Amongst the muniments and records left from the old days, was a picturesque record of some of the more modern men of Dunwich. On one page of a MS. folio, covering some 150 years, appeared the following for 1709. "John Swatman: Bailiff.

Thomas Mills		His Mark.
Samuel Moor		His Mark.
James Horsman		His Mark.
Hugh Simmons		His Mark.

This account was allowed By Us who were present at ye Passing of this account."

It would appear that John Swatman, being the only man of the company who could write, entered his own name and those of his fellows, while they filled in their marks. The translation of this almost forgotten language is as follows. Thomas Mills was a shepherd and his sign is a pair of sheep shears. Samuel Moor was a rope maker, hence the coil. James Horsman was a hurdle maker, and his sign is a primitive fence. Hugh Simmons was a thatcher, and that was his comb.

Those marks are as picturesque as were the cobbled streets, the ancient houses and the old Moot Hall. True they have all gone, freemen and burgesses, trades and trademarks alike, swept into the sea. Yet their names live on, and the old drowned city echoes to their affirmations.

It is almost certain that Dunwich was a Roman station. If one considers the coast as coming within the defensive survey of the Roman occupiers, the circumstantial evidence would point to this. With Burgh Castle to the north, and the supposed Walton Castle to the south, it would be difficult not to believe such was the case. It has been identified as Sitomagus.

The Dunwich story really begins in the seventh century when, to a port which must have been in existence, came Sigebert to his kingdom. He had been living in exile in Gaul, when the death of his step-brother Eorpwald, murdered by Richbert, necessitated his return to claim the throne. With but little imagination one can picture this young man, tall and broad and fair, stepping ashore from one of those cockle-shells that passed as ships (such as that unearthed at Sutton Hoo) and making his way, attended by his followers, amid the hovels that clustered about the mouth of Dunwich River. He was a member of the East Anglian royal house of the Uffingas, whose most illustrious son was Redwald (Sigebert's uncle or step-father). It is almost certain that Redwald kept his palace at Rendlesham.

Sigebert was soon followed by another young man, a Burgundian missionary monk, who was to become the first Bishop of Dunwich. His name was Felix, and the young king had met him in Gaul. It is naturally conjectured that Sigebert built himself a palace in Dunwich and probably a church for Felix.

The latter was not the only teacher who came to Dunwich at the King's request, for in all probability Furseus, an Irish monk of noble birth, came here and a school was set up. It is interesting to note that this is the earliest reference to the foundation of a

Snape Maltings

The moated Hall at Parham

Fishing in the River Deben at Ufford

Harrowing at Parham

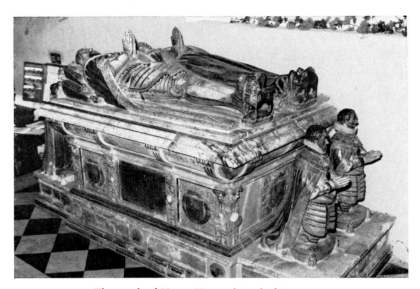

The tomb of Henry Howard, Earl of Surrey, in
Framlingham Church

Flatford Lock

Erwarton Gatehouse

The belfry in a churchyard at East Bergholt

school in England, and some have seen in it the beginnings of Cambridge University.

The new capital was not allowed to remain in peace for long; Sigebert with his brother Ecric was killed by Penda, the pagan king of Mercia. He was succeeded by Anna, whom we have already seen was killed by this same Penda.

The original extent of Dunwich must have been considerable, always bearing in mind that a medieval city was not large, and that London was contained within a square mile. Tradition has it that a forest called Eastwood stretched several miles south-east of the town, but was early devoured of the sea.

Dunwich came into prominence in the reign of King John, who gave it the first charter, thereby creating it a free borough. This was no mean favour, and for it the town paid 200 marks and 5,000 eels. The charter was confirmed again in his later years.

One church existed in the time of Edward the Confessor, but two more sprang up between then and Domesday, in fact six have been definitely traced: SS. Leonard, Peter, John, Martin, Nicholas and All Saints. Add to these the one founded by Felix, making seven. Gardner, the local historian, quotes two more, SS. Michael and Bartholomew, referred to but once as having been swallowed by the sea before 1331. To these may be added three chapels, those of SS. Anthony, Francis and Katherine; convents of the Franciscans and Dominicans; the Lazar Hospital of St. James, Maison Dieu or Holy Trinity; the Temple or Preceptory of Knights' Templars, which was a round church similar in character to the Temple Church in London.

The monastery of the Franciscans is the most interesting of the remaining ruins left. Its continuous grey walls, almost intact, and two beautiful gateways, form a memorial to a departed glory. The large gate served as the principal entrance to the house, while the lesser was for ordinary folk going to and from the chapel. There was evidently another gate in the east wall that has been destroyed. This enclosure has been taken over by the Ministry of Works.

The ancient apse of the Lazar chapel of St. James is eastward of the present parish church. The walls are ornamented with small intersecting arches of 22-inch radius, which is peculiar to Saxon and Norman architecture. It is now used as a mausoleum of the Barne family.

All Saints was the last of the old churches to disappear and, as a ruin on the cliff, was for many generations a picturesque and familiar sight. The steeple was maintained by Trinity House as a landmark for ships and when it was in danger of falling, a blacksmith from Westleton was commissioned to fasten iron bands round it. A not too easy task for a village craftsman, but one that was tackled and accomplished in the ordinary course of work.

The last service was held about 1755. The east-end disappeared over the cliff in February 1904, and the steeple on 12th November 1919, having stood sentinel during the years of the First World War. The last remaining buttress of the steeple was taken down, stone by stone, and re-erected in the churchyard of the modern St. James. However, it nearly came to grief when a German bomb fell just behind it in the Second World War.

Dunwich provided ships for the Royal Navy under several monarchs, many of the vessels being built in its own shipyards. It also sent a fleet to the Iceland fishing for many years. These vessels were 'wafted' by the Royal Navy, otherwise they were at the mercy of pirates and usually failed to return. It had three lifeboats: the *John Keble*, maintained by the family and named after the author of the *Christian Year*, which was actually towed to church to be blessed; the *Anne Ferguson* and the *Lily Bird*.

Dunwich sent two members to Parliament from the time of Edward I. They were carried past the town hall, shoulder high, upon election. The last of these municipal houses forms the oldest inhabited buildings in the main street. In common with other pocket boroughs it was disfranchised in 1832.

> There is a glorious City in the Sea,
> The sea is in the broad, the narrow streets,
> Ebbing and flowing. . . .
> No track of men, no footsteps to and fro,
> Lead to her gate.   Samuel Rogers.

It is a long way round by road to Sizewell, which is hardly a village. Names like the Cache Cliff at Minsmere, Sizewell Gap and

Minsmere Level conjure up memories of encounters and 'runs' almost too numerous to mention. This one-time fishing village, with an erection on the beach adorned with the name-boards of vessels presumably lost at sea, is no more. It has become a hand-maid of modern science, a nuclear power station.

We will skirt Orford with all its pomp and circumstance, and stop at Halvergate Island, where avocets have returned to breed in Suffolk after an absence of 150 years. These graceful, white and black, long-beaked birds bred along our coast, then suddenly vanished. They are causing some concern amongst bird lovers, because having reached 100 nesting pairs they have begun dwindling again. A scientist is at work to try and solve the riddle.

4

The Villages of South-east Suffolk

> There's the lark in the morning
> She will rise up from her nest,
> And she'll mount the white air
> With the dew on all her breast.

WE might start this section with Bruisyard on the Alde, hard to find but worth the search. It has an interesting old church with ridge tiles and a round tower of great age. The ancient south chapel now serves as a vestry. Here was a college for priests, later changed into a nunnery by Maud, Countess of Ulster. And here was buried in great state the wife of Lionel, Duke of Clarence and Lord of Clare. Neither should Bruisyard Hall be missed, a noble and interesting red-brick pile, set amid trees, with a green sward approach. Now a farmhouse, it was once the home of the Rouses.

Rendham again has an honest-to-goodness chapel dated 1750, with stabling to match. The church has a bell from the Bury foundry, with the inscription which means: "Lead us crowned Virgin to the blessed realms".

Sweffling has a rather nice flint-panelled south porch, with three niches above the doorway. But its greatest treasure is a boiled leather *(cuir bouilli)* cylindrical case, 11 inches high and 6 in diameter. It is elaborately tooled, evidently for a guild cup or chalice.

Benhall really consists of two detached villages called Benhall Green and Benhall Street. The church of St. Mary is filled with nineteenth-century box pews, which gives it an old-world atmosphere. Recently a bronze head of the Emperor Claudius was sold for £15,500 at Sothebys to a dealer acting on behalf of the British Museum. This superb head was found in 1907 by a small boy in the River Alde, where it passes through the grounds of Benhall Lodge. It has been suggested it belonged to a statue that may have been set up in Colchester, the Roman town sacked by the forces of Queen Boudicca in A.D. 61.

Sternfield is well known to members of our Royal Family because Major Sir Arthur Penn, secretary to the Queen Mother, had his home there. The Queen usually stays there when visiting Suffolk. The church possesses a good altar-piece in a painting by West of the "Blind restored to Sight".

Friston has a notable windmill, although now with only two sails. It was in the hands of the Reynolds family for many years, twizzling in the Suffolk sun. The present owner is desirous of demolishing it, which would be a great loss to the landscape and the atmosphere of the village. In the church, which is set on rising ground, is a fine specimen of wood carving in the Arms of James I cut from timbers 5 inches thick. Its restoration is a splendid tribute to a diligent parish church council. The tower is fine, on the upper part are traceried niches as large as windows.

Mention, too, must be made of Friston Chapel, known for miles around. It is a characteristic piece of country and non-conformist architecture peculiar to these parts, another being at Fressingfield. It is coffin-shaped (or is it pentagonal?), the idea being that all seats face towards the baptistry, and dates from the early part of the nineteenth century.

We must not miss the twin churches of Farnham and Stratford St. Andrew, in different parishes but within sight and sound of one another. Each possesses an early window.

There are at least two Saxmundhams, the original township of Samundeham, Saxmondham, Saymundham, that lines the bit of the Queen's highway of the A12, or the new which in most part lies discreetly westward of the railway station. But it is the old of which we think, that stretches back into the Domesday survey. when Roger Bigod, Algar (King Edward's thane), and Ranulf held the manors.

In the old days the Yarmouth Mail stopped at the 'Bell' four times a day at six in the morning and three in the afternoon down, and eleven in the morning and nine in the evening up. The *Shannon* between Colchester and Halesworth called at the 'Bell' as did the original *Blue*. When the railway came in 1856, the *Old Blue* finished its days in the Bell Yard.

This brings us to the church "that topped the neighbouring hill". A Suffolk church of flintwork, with curious and interesting pre-Reformation features, in font, decorated windows that light the road, piscina and inscription in English black letters. And whilst here, in the green shade, note that interesting headstone to a Saxmundham Noller, with sundial cut in the back and face, to tell the passing time which has been so kind to this Auburn.

Henry Bright the water-colour artist, who became a member of the Norwich School, was born here. His father made those grandfather clocks that ticked sonorously in so many local cottages; and the family lived at Park Cottage. When the home was sold up in 1871, some of the pictures in "handsome gilt frames" fetched mouth-watering prices. For example, a "Beautiful landscape Painting with Cattle, by Cuyp" fetched £2 15s. and another by the same artist, £3 5s.; a "Fishing Scene" by Stannard, £3; "A beautiful Miniature Painting by Hogarth", £3 3s.; "Dutch Peasants by H. Bright", £3 3s.; "Landscape in oils, Village Scene, by Stannard", £2 5s. But "Landscape, an exquisite Painting by H. Bright" fetched as much as £4 10s. What would they fetch today?

And they had tea in the market place when our Queen was crowned, just as they did at the Jubilee of Queen Victoria, and so many other national occasions before.

So to Framlingham, once the centre of great events; now it has let the world go by and remained itself, a lovely conglomeration of a little town. If in part it is the scene of England's story, it was also, according to Evelyn, "famous for producing the tallest and largest oak trees, perhaps in the world".

As one might expect the church is notable, not so much for its architectural features as for the treasures which it holds. Here are the richest tombs in the county, some removed from Thetford Priory at the Dissolution and placed in the chancel, which was built for the purpose. Among these is that of Henry Howard, Earl of Surrey, the poet, and Frances his wife. He was beheaded only a week prior to the death of Henry VIII, in token of which his coronet lies by his side. He appears in trunk hose, cap and jacket of bright-red velvet as in his portrait at Hampton Court. Behind kneel the three daughters—Jane, who married the Earl of Westmoreland; Katherine, who married Lord Berkeley, and Margaret, wife of Lord Scroop of Bolton—dressed in red robes, ermine collars and ruffs. In front are the two sons: Thomas, fourth Duke of Norfolk, and Henry Earl of Northampton.

In the north-east corner is a magnificent tomb of two of the three wives of Thomas, fourth Duke of Norfolk, Earl Marshal of England, who was beheaded on Tower Hill, 1572; neither can this generation be sure of which two it is. It is adorned with coats-of-arms and antlered stags. Adjoining is the tomb of Henry Fitzroy, Duke of Richmond, natural son of Henry VIII and Lady Elizabeth Talbot. This also bears shields of arms and, round the sides in a lively frieze, are scenes from Genesis, set out in engaging simplicity and frankness.

The tomb of Thomas Edward, third Duke, father of Surrey the poet, who escaped a like fate with his son owing to the death of Henry, is on the south side of the altar. He died 1554 and lies with Anne his wife, daughter of Edward IV. He wears a spade beard, and an antlered stag lies at their feet. Hanging high on the walls of the sanctuary is the helmet worn by Lord Thomas Howard, son of the Earl of Surrey, when he commanded the English forces at Flodden.

Among these rich tombs is that of Sir Robert Hitcham, who distinguished himself by endowing an almshouse for old men and women, and also buying Framlingham Castle from the Duke of Norfolk in 1635 for £14,000. Dying the next year he bequeathed it all to Pembroke College, Cambridge, to hold in trust for the poor. His almshouse seat in the church is an interesting bit of cabinet making, on which presumably the sexes sat back to back. His arms are on the poppy heads.

Another treasure in the church is an organ built after the Restoration by Thamar of Peterborough for Pembroke College.

The case is one of the only eight that have survived the destruction of such things by the Puritans and dates from about 1580, and Thamar was commissioned to build a new organ inside it. It was presented to Framlingham in 1704. Nailed on the back is the front of another early organ.

The organ was placed on a gallery at the west end, where M. R. James says it produced the best effect. It was afterwards moved to the floor of the church. The gallery, which was too good to destroy and was of the same period and style as the reredos at the east end, was placed in the hall at the castle.

About seven years ago the Ministry of Works decided that the gallery was out of place in the castle and ordered its removal. It has been replaced in the church and reunited with the organ at the west end. This splendid instrument has lately been rebuilt, which with the restoration of the gallery cost £9,000.

Framlingham Castle, built originally by the Bigods, was ordered to be taken down by Alnoth, a royal engineer in 1196. It seems to have been the proud possession of many Earls of Suffolk. Thomas Plantagenet, surnamed de Brotherton, repaired the damage sustained during Bigod's ownership, before it passed on to William de Ufford. It then came to John Mowbray and afterwards to the Howards.

The walls of grey stone and black flints, crowned by thirteen massive towers, are 40 feet high, and at some places 8 feet thick. From the large number of fireplaces, the remains of which can be seen at various levels, the castle must have been a forest of chimneys. Seven only remain, of finely moulded brick, and by reason of access to the walls can be studied at fairly close range. One of the tallest portions is the gate tower which was built by Thomas Howard in the reign of Henry VIII. The castle was dismantled in the seventeenth century.

Many a tale hangs over Framlingham and many a secret passage has been allowed to its hidden depths. Yet still the walls, towering above its sedgy moat, add interest and romance to the scenery and the quiet character of a delightful town.

Earl Soham is a large, pretty and straggling village, full of open spaces, set in a rolling landscape studded with the oaks that once made Suffolk a famous place for shipbuilding. The Lodge is an eighteenth-century moated house, probably erected on the site of the ancient manor house. On a buttress of the tower of the church, erected *c.* 1470, are tablets to Thomas Edward, the builder, and Ralph Colnett his assistant.

Cretingham has a delightful little church, unspoiled, with a hammer-beam roof. Munro Cautley bids visitors to notice the ridge tiles on the cottage immediately north of the churchyard, with a herdsman driving home two cows.

For anyone who is a lover of old churches, Great Glemham holds much of interest. It has a fine roof, besides other good features, but its chief pride is a Seven Sacrament Font, the panels of which are still in a good state of preservation. The sacraments are carved on a rayed background showing traces of colour, which is a device repeated at Woodbridge. In the panel for Mass the chalice can be seen on the altar, and the devil escaping from the shriven in that for Penance. The christmatory appears in Confirmation and Extreme Unction. This ark-like box held the three oils used in the sacraments. The shaft of the font is decorated with lily pots.

In the belfry are three Brasyer bells of the fifteenth century, inscribed—"This bell is made in the praise of all good saints". "May this ring be blessed by the good office of the Baptist," and "I am, when rung, called Mary the Rose of the world".

Parham Hall, now a farmhouse, was probably built by Sir Christopher Willoughby and dates from the fifteenth century. It was the home of Peregrine Lord Willoughby of Eresby and Parham, who distinguished himself in the wars of the Low Countries. This romantic old pile is noted for its high-pitched gables and original brick mullioned oriels, still arched and cusped, that have their feet in the greenish waters of the moat. It is approached by a Tudor gateway of old red brick, on which appear a wild man (as on the Suffolk fonts) and what looks like something out of a medieval bestiary. The courtyard side is a curious collection of plaster erections that shine picturesquely above the level lawns. Inside the Hall is a black oak staircase that must compare with the one at Crow's Hall.

Parham was later the home of John Tovell, a rich yeoman

farmer, and his astringent wife. With them lived Sarah Elmy who was responsible for the visits of George Crabbe, then apprenticed, to a doctor at Woodbridge. It is recorded of Tovell that he hardly ever went to bed sober, but lived to a great age.

Here is a place to linger and watch the shadows come and go in timeless procession. In the moat, now dammed by causeways into ponds, are eels, pike and tench without number, too satisfied with their greeny depths to be tempted out by the bauble of a bait. Hard by the old gateway, set in the walls of an outbuilding, is the inscription *"Verite est sans peer"*.

An excellent description of the old house is given by Crabbe's son in his biography of his father, when he was taken there on holiday: "On entering the house there was nothing at first sight to remind one of the farm—a spacious hall paved with blue and white marble—and at one extremity a very handsome drawing-room, and at the other a fine old staircase of black oak, polished till it was slippery as ice. . . . No noise was heard, except the melancholy and monotonous cooing of a turtle dove varied, however, by the shrill treble of a canary."

Parham village, so ideally situated in peace, is noted for its pretty cottage gardens and also for the flowering thorn that blooms at Christmas. Until recently here was one of those long tenures of village post offices, broken by the retirement of Mr. Royden H. Frost after a century of service by his family.

Easton on the Deben was the seat of the Duke of Hamilton, and is really a lovely spot, still unspoiled. Munro Cautley says the church exhibits the curious taste of the eighteenth century because the park wall was built up to the western tower and enclosed the north porch so as to give private entrance for the noble owners. There are three interesting brasses in the chancel, one to John Brook, 1426, and another to John Wingfield, 1584, who is in armour. The third is to Radcliff Wingfield, 1601, in ruff and brocaded petticoat. The fifteenth-century Brasyer bell is inscribed: "Now Gabriel being sent, bears joyful tidings to holy Mary".

Through Marlesford comes an exceptionally pretty piece of main road, skirting the park of Little Glemham Hall. It is Suffolk at its very best and leaves a memory of pastoral peace. The Hall, seen at the end of an avenue of trees, is not suggestive of beauty because of alterations that have rendered it into a barracky-looking brick house. However, it has a goodly array of windows to relieve the severity. When it was the home of the Glemhams it was a very different place and, according to an old painting, resembled what we now know as Knole in Kent. It was altered by a Dudley North, born 1684, whose initials on the rain-water heads, dated 1722, probably give a clue to the time when this was effected.

What it lacked in former exterior interest, it certainly made up in internal furnishings when the Norths filled it with their fine and contemporary pieces, some of which were probably moved from their London house. These included the famous Sate Bed of gilded amorini, hung with rich velvets, tasselled and fringed, and six equally magnificent chairs to match. This apartment was also hung with gorgeous Mortlake tapestries. The furniture ranged from the Stuart to the late Georgian period.

In the church is a brass which sheds some light on the origin of the term 'silly' as applied to Suffolk people, which really signifies holy or wise:

> This sylly grave the ashes under hyde
> Of Thomas Glemham Sonn to Christopher.

Snape has become a village of world-wide fame. Long years ago the Augustinians had a priory which was really a cell to Colchester. Even now the little church set on a hill by the cross-roads contains a very beautiful font. Up to the turn of the century Dunningworth Horse Fair was held here in the month of August. Then, at the commencement of his career Benjamin Britten lived in the mill.

But Snape really came into modern fame through the maltings, which Newson Garrett bought as a coal and corn warehouse at Snape Bridge. Within three years of his arrival he was shipping 17,000 quarters of barley each year to London and other markets. This enterprising but irascible man was the father of the first woman doctor, who was also the first woman mayor of Aldeburgh; and of Millicent Fawcett, the wife of the blind Postmaster-General. He built the very pleasant line of buildings adjacent to the old humped-back bridge, demolished in 1959. In those days the river scene was made picturesque by the spreading sails of the barges, the Alde being navigable as far as this.

However, the greater fame of the Maltings (really in Tunstall as far as boundaries go) came when Benjamin Britten turned the main building into a concert hall of the most modern and unique type, to house the Aldeburgh Festival. This was opened by the Queen in 1967 and cost nearly £180,000. Then, on the first night of the festival in 1969, this wonderful achievement was destroyed by fire. However, such is enterprise, that a new hall was ready and opened by the Queen on 5th June 1970, with a concert of "Music fit for a Queen".

Campsey Ashe was the home of the Priory of Austin Nuns, established as long ago as 1195. The fifteenth-century water mill, which once formed an essential part of the domestic economy and independence of the priory, is a weather-boarded structure built of ancient materials, much like an old ship, and still has its original machinery.

> I loved the brimming wave that swam
>   Thro' quiet meadows round the mill,
> The sleeping pool above the dam,
>   The pool beneath it never still,
> The meal sacks on the whiten'd floor,
>   The dark round of the dripping wheel,
> The very air about the door
>   Made misty by the floating meal.
>
> Tennyson.

Tunstall has a church with a fine tower, rather badly restored, which provided a pattern for a tower at Walberswick according to the ancient agreement still preserved. Also here was a Particular Baptist Chapel of some fame that could command a congregation of 400 in such an out-of-the-way place. The inn has the delightful designation of the 'Plough and Sail'. This is the Sandling area and much of the land has been given over to forestry.

Iken, remote from the world of stress and strain, is in a lovely position. The church stands on a hill on the south side of a bend in the Alde. If this is not a defensive position it is certainly the most picturesque in the county. One imagines it should have a round tower, instead of which it is square. This has become a place of speculation because the ancient church is dedicated to St. Botolph, who, coupled with Jurmin, was a great ecclesiastical figure. In an adjoining chapel at Bury all his relics were preserved. He has been identified as the Abbot of Ikanloe, and this monastery may well have been at this very Iken, in this lovely secluded spot.

Wickham Market also stands on a hill, and the church of All Saints was described as a conspicuous sea-mark. It has an unusual octagon tower, with an external sanctus bell cote and is on the old Yarmouth turnpike, now the A12. Once upon a time there was an ironworks here that made steam engines, water wheels, windmills and machinery more especially adapted for corn and flour mills. Then Mr. James White of this town had a self-winding clock, never requiring to be wound up. The 'White Hart', altered from 'The Harte' in the time of Henry VII, is one of the most ancient inns in the county.

Letheringham had another religious establishment in a priory of Augustinians. This priory, of which no ruin remains, stood on the north side of the parish church; the site is now a stackyard. The church had a number of fine brasses and Munro Cautley says: "Apparently a hundred years ago every collector pillaged this church and some of them were the neighbouring clergy."

But Letheringham Mill, between Wickham Market and Easton, reminds us that there has been a watermill on the site since the days of King Harold. It is mentioned in Domesday as being part of the Manor of Letheringham. The last lord of the manor, the Duke of Hamilton and Brandon, sold it in 1921. Situated in a curve of the Deben it has a park-like water meadow which is most peaceful and attractive, the home of a variety of ducks, geese, guinea- and pea-fowl.

The mill was in working order until sixty years ago, when the machinery was dismantled and installed in Kelsale windmill. In 1696 it was the scene of a brutal murder when a servant, Jonah Snell, murdered the miller, John Bullard, and his son, with an axe. Snell was hanged in Potsford Wood, nearby, where the remains of the gibbet still stand.

Charsfield has a pub called the 'Three Horseshoes', and the carved beam dated 1585 in the ringers' gallery at the church came out of the dismantled Elizabethan rectory. Dallinghoo St. Mary has a central tower, and Petistree church has a brass with effigies of John Bacon and his two wives, 1580.

Boulge has one immortal memory, that of Edward FitzGerald. The family came to live at the Hall, a house dating from the reign of Queen Anne, which had by the park gates a quaint little one-storeyed thatched cottage. Of this FitzGerald eventually took possession. Here came all kinds of people including the 'Wits of Woodbridge'. Notwithstanding, he looked upon Boulge as one of the ugliest and dullest places in England. For constant companions he had a cat, dog and his parrot Beauty Bob.

From Boulge cottage, where his best work was done, it is a short walk to the church with its well-established rookery. And it was here his body was brought back to rest under a stone, inscribed:

Edward Fitzgerald.

Born 31st March, 1809. Died 14th June, 1883.

It is He that hath made us, and not we ourselves.

There are the remains of a rose tree on the grave: "This Rose Tree raised in Kew Gardens from Seed Brought by William Simpson, Artist-Traveller from the Grave of Omar Khayyam at Naishapur was planted by a few Admirers of Edward FitzGerald in the name of the Omar Khayyam Club, October, 1893."

Bredfield was his birthplace and this is what he wrote about the old Jacobean home:

> Some of the tall ash trees about it used to be visible at sea; but I think their topmost branches are decayed now. . . . I like the idea of the old English house holding up its inquiring chimneys and weathercocks (there is a great physiognomy in weathercocks) towards the far-off sea, and the ships upon it. How well I remember when we used all to be in the Nursery and from the windows see the hounds come across the lawn, my father and Mr. Jenny in their hunting-caps, etc., with their long whip—all Daguerreotyped into the mind's eye now—and that is all.

Incidentally FitzGerald was the maiden name of his imperious mother, taken over by his father when her father died.

Ufford, with the stocks at the lychgate of its beautiful church, holds much within to speak of days of splendour and pride. It is a village of winding ways, serene and sylvan, holding fragrant mellowed homesteads that seem to stay the hand of Time. It is indeed a treasure tucked away from fretting fingers. Long years ago Sir John de Peyton's younger son, who had crusaded with Edward I and was a Justiciary of Ireland, took this spot as his name and became Robert de Ufford.

In the church is a font cover, considered the finest specimen in the whole country, dating from the fourteenth century. This tapers up tier on tier to the roof, from which it is suspended by a Pelican in her Piety. Tabernacle work with open tracery, at one time painted and gilded, was made in the witchery of craftsmanship to be telescopic, but is now triptych in form. Even Dowsing the iconoclast is alleged to have declared it a glorious cover.

Rendlesham, according to Fuller, was "a remarkable place I assure you, which, though now a country village, was anciently the residence of the kings of the East Angles; wherein king Redwald, a mongrel Christian kept at the same time . . . the communion table, and altars for idols". In 1687 a silver crown was dug up here, and as quickly melted down to the eternal despair of all archaeologists. Rendlesham House was burnt down twice, the second time in 1898, and after being the home of the Rendlesham family for centuries became that of the famous Peter Isaac Thellusson. Two gateways in the form of Follies remain.

Wantisden church tower is built of coralline crag. A spiral staircase leads to the 'monk's room', where, it is supposed, the priest taught aspirants for the monastic life. The Black Death appears to have destroyed the village in 1349. Old people used to call a certain enclosure 'The bow and arrow place'; it is now known as 'The Old Yards'.

Butley is famous for the remains of the Augustinian Priory founded by Ranulph de Glanville in 1171. Of the priory buildings only one arch and two pillars are now left. However, the gateway has been turned into an interesting and curious-looking dwelling.

This was carried out by a certain George Wright in 1737, who put in a fine Georgian staircase. The carriageway has been turned into a single apartment, measuring 33 feet by 24 feet—a really magnificent arched room. By this transformation the glorious span of flush-work, enshrining a great armorial of thirty-five shields of the great Suffolk families, has been preserved. Happily, too, it survived the enormous bomb that fell directly in front of the southern face, and left a crater too deep for belief.

Within a mile of the priory is Staverton Forest, a medieval relic, unique and rare. Something short of a square mile in area, it holds many massive oaks and gigantic hollies. At Eastertide it is a sea of daffodils. From these woods the Pilgrims' Way leads to the priory, lined with trees planted in fives for the Five Wounds. Neither must we omit to mention the famous 'Butt ond Oyster', butt being a small fish and not a barrel as one might suppose.

Both Wantisden and Chillesford church towers are built of the rare coralline crag, the oldest geological deposit in England. This was a great area for sheepwalks, where snipe keep up their drumming and nightingales their song. Sudbourne Hall, now demolished, was a famous sporting centre and venue for poaching. Boyton is a parish near Butley Water, as also Capel St. Andrew. At the former was Frog's Hall Farm, but if connected with *Toad of Toad Hall*, I do not know.

Of the greatest significance to the archaeologist was the unearthing in 1939 of the Sutton Hoo ship burial, with all its fantastic treasures that have been almost definitely linked with the Royal House of the Uffingas. Sutton Hoo is only 5 miles from Rendlesham. This ship-burial formed one of several barrows, and there is little doubt it was the burial ground of the royal house. From the hoard of coins found it dates from 650–670 A.D. This is what R. L. S. Bruce Mitford says: "Let us remember, the Sutton Hoo grave is not just any ordinary chieftain's tomb, but a phenomenon of the first magnitude, even against the European background." As the tomb contained no evidence of a body it must be looked upon as a cenotaph.

By the richness and size of the ship, it might have been the one described in Beowulf. Moreover, it has been suggested that the

Letheringham Mill

Two river scenes: *(above)* Flatford Mill and *(below)* Holbrook Mill

Nacton in autumn

Stour House, East Bergholt

Higham

jewellery found therein may have been made by a royal goldsmith working at the court of the Saxon king at Rendlesham, and that the cloisonné jewellery was of local origin. Speculation has inclined toward Aethelhere, killed at Winwaed, Yorkshire, in 655, or his brother Aethelwald, as being the body so honoured.

Shottisham, a delightful wayside village, has an inn called the 'Sorrel Horse'. Coprolite was dug here. Bromeswell is famous for a Mechlin bell inscribed: "Jesus am I, cast by Cornelis Wagherens in the year of our Lord, 1530." Eyke has a fine Norman arch and a central tower. The wards of the church key form the word IKE. The inn is the 'Elephant and Castle', I know not why.

We now move to the Carlford and Colneis hundreds beginning with Otley, a beautiful clean and green village. The clerestoried church has some good bench ends, one bearing the arms of the Gosnold family, who once occupied the lovely old moated Hall. Both Burgh and Culpho churches are dedicated to St. Botolph. The former is picturesquely situated at the top of a steep bank, identified as part of a Roman encampment, as its name would imply. Thistleton Hall, about a mile away, is double moated. Grundisburgh Hall was once the seat of the Blois family whom we met at Yoxford. Another timbered house is 'Basts'. The church has a fine roof and beautiful screen. Hasketon church has a round tower. Great Bealings, situated in a finely wooded district on the river Finn, was the birthplace of Sir Thomas Seckford, founder of Woodbridge School. He also provided the first set of county maps, done by Christopher Saxton at his expense. Tuddenham St. Martin has an extremely interesting church, containing good woodwork in roof, bench ends and pulpit.

At Playford's moated Hall once lived, for nearly thirty years, Thomas Clarkson, 'The Friend of Slaves' and a co-worker with Wilberforce. He died there in 1846 and an obelisk in the churchyard has been erected to his memory. The church possesses a magnificent Standing Cup and a splendid brass to Sir George Felbrigg, of the camail period, with basinet and arms on jupon, dating from 1400.

Martlesham has moved into folk-lore by reason of its inn sign— "As red as Martlesham Lion". This old figure-head is said to have come from a Dutch warship taken at the battle of Sole Bay. The inn was an old coaching inn where the mail was stored in a strong-room when in transit from London to Yarmouth. Inside is a curi-ous ceiling. The church, set amid trees on rising ground overlook-ing a backwater of the Deben, was for long served by the Doughty family. Their pew was made from the ancient screen. This peaceful God's acre was once the scene of body snatchers.

Waldringfield, the Walringafelda of Domesday, has been trans-lated as meaning the field of the sons of Waldhere, or a family settlement. Coprolites were dug here, in great quantity, and there is a coprolite window in the church. The Waller family have held the living for well over a century. Since those days, it has become a yachtsman's paradise, difficult to see the water for the boats.

Newbourne was famous for giants, George Page and his brother Meadows. George stood 7 feet 7 inches in his stockinged feet and is buried beside the church path, under an inscription that reads: "Sacred to the memory of George Page, the Suffolk Giant, who died April 20th. 1870. The deceased was exhibited in most towns in England, but his best exhibition was with his blessed Re-deemer." When he finally settled down he married a very short woman.

It is thought that the 'Fox' was built of old ships' timbers, be-cause the bolt holes remain. Every Whit Wednesday crowds from surrounding villages would come to frolic here, dancing to the music of an accordion and there would be bowling for a copper kettle every Whit Monday.

The special feature of the church is a rare graffito (scratch draw-ing) of a medieval three-masted ship, c. 1450–1500, on the western jamb of the south porch.

Brightwell is indeed a happy spot, in a green valley of the Mill river, so named from a fulling mill, with a gem of a church and the old Georgian vicarage set each side of the hill. According to Skeat it derived from a bright or clear well. The Barnardistons lived at the Hall (now no more), and it is their armour that hangs in the church, two tilting helmets, sword, gauntlets and spurs. The crested helmets, which have been newly restored to their original colours, bear a bittern standing amid bulrushes.

The church of St. John Baptist is quite unique and was known as Brightwell Chapel. It was almost in ruins when Thomas Essington had it remodelled about 1656. It was he who had those delightful brick obelisks placed in position on the four corners and the east gable of the roof. He also had the two unusual monuments erected to the memory of his children, the work of a German artist.

Bucklesham has an inn called 'The Shannon', advisedly so because of the Broke family who held the advowson of the church, and their home at Nacton.

Once upon a time and not so long ago, Kirton possessed two pubs, the 'White Horse' and the 'Greyhound'. Now alas, and only yesterday, the older of the two, the 'Greyhound', also known as 'The Dog', has entirely vanished. In the old days you might have met with 'Whistling Jim'. When he was taken in hand by the parson who intended exhibiting him at a local fête, he was prompt to declare he couldn't whistle on milk.

And so we come to Falkenham, approaching it down the sloping village street, overhung by giant cedar trees, until we arrive at the 'Dog'. This old inn is traditionally connected with smuggling, and indeed it would be remakable if it were not so. Drunkards' Lane leads to Kirton. Falkenham post mill was dismantled about 1918. The church of St. Ethelbert has a fine embattled tower.

Although two distinct parishes, Trimley St. Martin and Trimley St. Mary are always spoken of as one. This has become more apparent with the uniting of the two benefices. Indeed so ancient is the history of these parishes and the immediate vicinity that two others within their borders, now lost in the mists of time, were those of Allston or Alston and Stratton, each with a church. The two churches are erroneously stated as being in one churchyard, but such is not really the case. A ditch, now nearly levelled, separates them. Nevertheless they provide an extremely interesting picture, standing as they do beside the Ipswich-Felixstowe road.

Opposite is the 'Three Mariners', a very old house that has had a new look. Of the name there is a variety of opinions, but it seems reasonable to assume that the three Cavendish ships—*The Desire, Hugh Gallant* and *Content*—had something to do with it. Needless to say there were local curios among the customers, one being Mrs. Garnham, a keen fisherwoman, who caught eels. "I go down there when the river is frozen for preference. The cold weather brings them up."

Thomas Cavendish, born at Grimston Hall, was baptized at Trimley St. Martin on 19th September 1560. He was the second person to circumnavigate the earth, looting and burning Spanish ships. Amongst his men were Mr. John Way, the preacher; Mr. Thomas Fuller of Ipswich, the pilot; and Mr. Francis Pretty of Eyke, who wrote the history of the adventure. Cavendish was lost on the next voyage, dead at 30.

We now cross the Orwell for our next hundred, that of Samford. It is good to think this includes areas on both banks of the Orwell, from Harwich harbour to the outskirts of Ipswich, and the north bank of the Stour from Orwell Haven to Seafield Bay, as a wild-life haven. We will begin with Erwarton.

This little village at the base of land between Orwell and Stour has a great deal of interest. First the Hall, built 1575, with an almost eccentric gatehouse of brick, looking like a piece of ancient furniture with legs in the air. It is said, and not without founda-tion, that Anne Boleyn used to visit here when the Calthorpes made it their home. It was also a tradition that her heart was buried in the chancel of the church. When alterations and restora-tions were carried out in 1837, a heart-shaped casket was found and reburied. This suggests that oral tradition cannot be lightly dismissed. The church is of interest because of the Davillers' tombs. The earliest effigy is of a cross-legged knight, probably Sir Bartholomew Davillers, who died 1287.

Chelmondiston, set on a rise, is a pretty spot but its attraction for all lovers of the water is at Pin Mill, once upon a time a great centre for barges and bargees. Here is another 'Butt and Oyster'. Although the best barges were made at Harwich, Thames barges were also made here, and it has been the centre for barge races, of which at one time there were two a year. When the famous Roman Cement was made, septaria was dredged from the river at this point. Not far removed is Butterman's Bay, the deepest part of the Orwell.

Holbrook is a village noted for its beauty, situated on a bay of that name by the Stour. A tributary runs through its midst and was not unknown to smuggling. Here is the Royal Hospital School, removed from Greenwich in 1933. Not so long ago, at the little shop by the mill, a kindly man had some tame eels and trout in the stream that ran under his house. And not least was a budgerigar that talked unceasingly of 'Willy Buster' the dog. To see the eels come for their sour milk which he kept for their delight, and one brute seize the tail of another, was a sight indeed.

The tower of the church contains a lot of septaria, obviously dredged from the river. There is a double piscina, but the feature is the Consecration Crosses, within and without.

Woolverstone church, in the beautiful park of 400 acres, is one of the most lovely spots in the county. When I was there, the churchyard was kept to perfection, with clipped yews and finely mown grass, by an old man who looked part of the scene and something out of Gray's *Elegy*.

This was the home of the Berners family. The Hall was built in 1776 by a William Berners, who owned the London street of that name. It is now a boarding grammar school for boys under the Inner London Education Authority. The church was rebuilt by a Mrs. Berners, who placed a window within to the memory of her parents, the Reverend Joshua and Mrs. Rowley. One of the old Mrs. Berners used to ride in her carriage drawn by four Suffolk Punches.

Wherstead was also noted for its beauty. F. Barham Zincke wrote up the history of the parish in no mean fashion, in 1887; he was then the incumbent. He dealt with its antiquities, the squires, local characters, poachers, dialect, flora, fauna and superstitions.

Sir Robert Harland built the Hall in 1792, Sir Jeffrey Wyatville being the architect. Zincke met Sir Robert in 1848 when he had received the price of the Orwell estate which he had just sold. He told the vicar—"There, I have in that pocket £111,000. I intend to spend the whole of it. If when I am dead and buried there is half-a-crown over, it will be enough." But he died within the year. At one time Wherstead had ten woods and was pre-eminent as a sporting estate. The Duke of Wellington came here to shoot and peppered one of the guns—to wit Lord Granville. About the only remark he made was to the effect that he shouldn't have got in the way. The church has a Norman doorway to the south porch. The inn is 'The Ostrich'.

So we pass to Copdock, which has an inn named the 'White Elm' and no village. The church of St. Peter has a fifteenth-century font and cover, and a squint in the north pier of the chancel arch.

Bentley once had an Augustinian priory at Dodnash in this parish, a name perpetuated in Dodnash Farm. Here was the first station in Suffolk coming from London, or the last going to London. It was a junction for the Hadleigh line, now alas no more. At one time it had a stationmaster.

> When William the Conqueror reigned with great fame,
> Bentley was my seat, and Tollemache my name.

Tattingstone is indivisible from its Wonder. The reason for this most unique Folly of two cottages disguised as a Gothic church seems to have been buried with Thomas White, who bought the manor in 1726 and rebuilt the Hall. Evidently his outlook needed uplift, so he erected this sham and gothicized the façade of his retainers' homes.

In the churchyard is a memorial to a William Talmash, which concludes: "An honest man's the noblest work of God". He was a parish clerk for nearly fifty years, and from his name could claim to be a member of the Bentley family.

But the beauty of Tattingstone, Stutton and Holbrook are threatened by the proposed reservoir which will drown so much, including the ancient and picturesque Alton Mill. Once destroyed, this lovely bit of England will have gone for ever.

Stutton is another beauty spot overlooking Harwich Harbour. The Hall was erected by Sir E. Jermy, and is remarkable for its chimneys, and a brick gateway akin to the one at Erwarton.

Brantham has a spice mill with a lovely smell, to make up for the ever-growing plastics manufacturers.

East Bergholt, on Suffolk's borderland, sets the scene and tone for the rest of the county, and has been described as the perfect English landscape. It may well be so for Constable himself said: "The beauty of the surrounding scenery, its gentle declivities, its luxuriant meadow flats sprinkled with flocks and herds, its well-cultivated uplands, its woods and rivers, with numerous scattered villages and churches, farms and picturesque cottages, all impart to this particular spot an amenity and elegance hardly anywhere else to be found." It is not too much to say it is the Englishman's dream of the ideal.

Constable was born there on 11th June 1776, of a family resident in the locality for several centuries. For a time he followed his father's trade as a miller; he even became known as 'the handsome young miller'. One of the mills was that of Flatford, which, together with Willy Lot's cottage, was all but in ruins not many years ago and might have gone the way of his own birthplace.

T. E. Hulme has said that nobody before Constable saw things, or at any rate painted them, in that particular way. And T. S. R. Boase in his *English Art* speaks of Constable's inspired power of observation, that his aim was to understand a landscape by constant study and by reproducing it in all its changing aspects. "In fact he is one of the most dedicated of painters. Today he is to many the greatest and best loved of English painters, and sometimes is acclaimed as the father of Impressionism." Boase goes on to speak of the skies of Constable's later period, from which it has been said the coming weather can easily be foretold. It must be realized that it was the French who acclaimed him, because the "Hay Wain" had been returned unsold from the Academy of 1821. But at the Salon of 1842 they said: "Look at these landscapes by an Englishman—the ground appears to be covered with dew."

East Bergholt church is of considerable interest. The tower is unfinished by reason, it is said, of sinister influences; but the great feature is the medieval wooden bell-cage standing detached in the churchyard.

One thing more, and that so characteristic of those days. It was said of Willy Lott, the possessor of Valley Farm in Constable's day, that "he was born in the house and that he passed more than 80 years without having spent four whole days away from it".

It should also be mentioned that Randolph Churchill lived in the village, and compiled the first volume of his illustrious father's biography there.

If we approach the Suffolk countryside, as did the Roman legions, we enter by Stratford St. Mary, and immediately the spirit that pervades it is upon us. In the coaching days it was here they changed horses. Before that the rich clothiers had their homes here; many of these still remain and have been faithfully and beautifully restored.

The church exhibits that fine flint-work, with inscriptions to the memory of the Mors or Morse family. In the churchyard is a memorial to "Anne Richardson, last remaining daughter of the celebrated author of Clarissa, Pamela and Sir Charles Grandison; obit December 27, 1803, aet 66." Richardson was the father of English novelists and lived at Hammersmith in a house later occupied by Burne-Jones the artist.

Of Holton St. Mary there is nothing to say, but of Higham it is rather different, as it is situated where the Stour and the Brett combine. And from its wooded slopes one can look out upon the delectable Dedham Vale. In 1930 at the Manor House, known as Barhams, wall paintings of an unusual character were found behind plaster. Dating from about 1600 and executed in red and black was a design of a flower and pomegranate, finished off with a frieze bearing verses of the Twenty-third Psalm. Higham is one of the prettiest of the villages in this part of Constable's country.

There are two Wenhams, but it is Little that contains the greater interest. Little Wenham Hall was built of Flemish bricks used in the time of Henry II, but without doubt they were imported. This is the earliest known example of their use in this country. It is one of the very few small castellated houses of the thirteenth century, with its hall and chapel. The latter has a vaulted roof and a beautiful window. The village church is assigned to the same builder. In this is a fine brass dated 1514 of a man in armour and wife in pedimented head-dress, Thomas Brewse. One of the fifteenth-century bench-ends with poppy head, formerly in Great Wenham church, is now in the Victoria and Albert Museum.

Capel St. Mary was a Suffolk village noted for its beauty. It was so named from an ancient chapel, and is situated in the vale of a small mill stream that falls into the Stour. Raydon church is an archaeologist's paradise, with buttresses and a thirteenth-century piscina with a double drain. Shelley on the Brett has a rather nice little church. Chattisham manor belongs to the Provost and Fellows of Eton College. Washbrook pub is 'The Brook', and the church has wonderful stone arcading in the chancel. At the base of the tower is a huge sarsen stone. Burstall church has a fourteenth-century north aisle with traceried windows.

Hintlesham has an H-shaped Hall, once belonging to the Timperleys. In the lovely grounds are beautiful trees, including an immense clipped yew. This became the home of Anthony Scott Stokes, who founded the Hintlesham Festival of Music and the Arts in 1950. His death in July 1970 has threatened the future of this institution of international fame.

5

The Margaret Catchpole Villages

Love warps the mind a little from the right.
Crabbe.

CLEMENT SHORTER in an introduction to an edition of the
story said: "*Margaret Catchpole, A Suffolk Girl*, is the classic
novel of Suffolk." He was perfectly correct, because it is so essentially local and so realistic of the life of the county that one is
always in a dilemma, when the name is mentioned, as to whether
the tale or the person is referred to. He goes on: "Margaret Catchpole is one of the few heroines of fiction of whom one loves to
remember that she was real flesh and blood." Moreover, the scene
is so conveniently localized, neither are the place-names disguised,
that we have in fact a Margaret Catchpole Country, as well as a
Constable Country, to vie with the Lorna Doone Country and the
Wessex Country of Thomas Hardy. Shorter suggests that three per-
sonalities interest us: the author, Richard Cobbold, the heroine
and the author's mother.

Mrs. Cobbold was born Knipe at Watling Street, London, about
1764. She first married a William Clarke in 1790, a Portman of
the borough and Comptroller of the Customs of Ipswich. He was
about 60 years of age, of very delicate health and died within six
months of the marriage. After a very short space of time she became
the second wife of John Cobbold of the Cliff Brewery, Ipswich,
then living at the family seat of Holywells. At the time of her marriage he was a widower with fourteen children living out of six-

teen. She was to add seven more to the quiver, six sons and one daughter, though they did not all survive.

It was rumoured that in her early days she was an actress, but there is no confirmation for this. Certainly she was a versifier, and Charles Dickens immortalized her as Mrs. Leo Hunter in *Pickwick Papers*, with a supposed example of her work, which was not unlike the reality:

> Can I view thee panting, lying
> On thy stomach, without sighing;
> Can I unmoved see thee dying
> On a log,
> Expiring frog!

Turning to Richard Cobbold—he has some eighteen books to his credit, but only one has survived by which his name is known, namely *Margaret Catchpole*. This country girl of village stock, who three times saved the life of a member of the Cobbold family, provided a first-class romance, the details of which could only have been known to him as a member of that family. He describes it as a true narrative, but, as Shorter remarks, "He possessed a genuine imaginative faculty", so he may have persuaded himself that it was so.

Margaret was the daughter of one Jonathan Catchpole, a labourer, then living in a tied cottage at Nacton, but her birth appears in the register at Hoo, near Framlingham. This fact must have been known to Cobbold but is not stated. Her father was working for a Mr. Denton, who bred the famous Suffolk carthorses. Jonathan had a team of them to look after and was the head ploughman on the estate. Like other little country girls Margaret was given rides on the backs of these lovely creatures, and as she grew up became as fearless as a Newmarket jockey.

The Catchpole Country really begins at Butley, near the ruins of the old abbey. Here lived the evil genius of the plot, Captain Bargood, in the Green Cottage, so called from the colour of its shutters. When not engaged in smuggling this was an ideal area for poaching, so that his men could be fully employed on the Marquis of Hertford's estate at Sudbourne.

The captain is described as a clever as well as desperate adventurer. He continued to keep up appearances as a steady trader, and had vessels that were regularly chartered. His sails visited, with proper invoices, all the ports along the coast and he had connexions in every town. Yet he had an undercurrent in the contraband trade which paid him far greater profits than his regular accounts.

Will Laud, who developed into Margaret's unworthy lover and became corrupted by the captain, was the son of Stephen Laud, described as a famous boatman, who for many years plied the ferry boat between Harwich and Landguard. It required a skilful pilot to manage such a boat, which had nearly 2 miles to run across the estuary. As government letters were always conveyed from Harwich to the Fort, the ferryman was in receipt of government pay. Stephen had been left a widower with one son, William, whom he apprenticed to a boat-builder at Aldeburgh. William, it was said, had studied navigation with a brother of Crabbe the poet.

John Luff, the next villain, is described as "gruff and surly looking, a fellow who seemed formed of such material as compose a cannon-ball. He looked like what he was, an iron-hearted and iron-fisted desperado, whose only pleasure was to serve a bad man, and to rule everyone in a ship who had a little more feeling than himself."

He is followed on the stage by Lieutenant Barry, a brave young sailor in the Preventive Service, second son of Mr. Henry Barry, a miller and farmer of Levington Hill, who was also in love with Margaret. Such was the cast of a tale that is really a period piece, with all its moralizing and extended dialogue, but nevertheless a good story. Moreover, it is undoubtedly a piece of romantic fiction.

Although Margaret lived at Nacton, the scene really becomes alive on the other side of the Deben—which is only natural. The *mise en scène* is contained in one small paragraph where the smugglers break company: "By twos and threes they dispersed, some to Boyton, some to Butley, some to Shottisham, Ramsholt, Bawdsey, Hollesley, Felixstowe, one or two as far as Trimley, Nacton and Ipswich." Some of these villagers we have already dealt with.

Hollesley had an excellent bay, in which Nelson sheltered his fleet, and which FitzGerald wrote:

> Saw victorious Nelson's topmasts
> Anchoring in Hollesley Bay.

It is here that the waters of the Alde find confluence with the sea, and it was here it was feared that Bonaparte might effect a landing if he ventured to invade England. Naturally enough it was a good place to land a load of contraband.

Of the church, this was one of the richest livings in Suffolk, held at one time by a son of the author of the romance in question, who was not only the rector, but one of the chief landowners. Those were the days when John Threadkell kept the 'Old Fox'.

When they ran the cargo, they would have gone through Alderton, a really delightful spot, especially so when the white sails of the mill twizzled in the sun and air. Here were most things a village required, including a policeman and a doctor. The noble church has a ruined tower, but inside is spacious grandeur. Amongst the rectors was a Giles Fletcher, brother of Phineas, and cousin to John Fletcher the dramatist. The epitaphs to be found here include one to the Reverend Robert Biggs, forty years rector, who died in 1769. "He was what is more truly valuable—An Honest Man."

If we travel westward and upward along a lonely bit of road, we come to Ramsholt with its unique church perched on the cliff above the river's bank. The tower is oval on plan, with three buttresses, north, south and due west. A good deal of septaria has been used in its construction. It has the old-fashioned box-pews, with a three-decker pulpit set in the midst, the pews east of the pulpit facing west. That the tower was built as a look-out seems highly probable. Below, tucked away safely from the world, is the inn now known as the 'Ramsholt Arms', but formerly the Dock Inn.

Naturally enough such a romantic spot figures in the tale. "While dashing through the sea, past the sand-bank, or bar, at the mouth of the Deben, those on board saw a solitary light burning in Ramsholt church, a sign that she might send a boat on shore in safety. Luff undertook to go. He did so, and found a messenger from Captain Bargood to land the cargo at the Eastern Cliff, as the coastguard had received information that a run was going to take place at Sizewell Gap, and they had therefore drawn away their men, that their force at the point might be strong enough."

It is not a long way back, through Alderton, to Bawdsey, which contained the famous *pied à terre* of the gang, rivalling *Treasure Island* in its fantasy. It might be mentioned that Bawdsey was a rare place for wrecks, which used to be placed in the manor barn near the Sun Inn—as it was called in Margaret's day—now closed. It is described as being situated in a "street of that long, sandy village of Bawdsey". It was in this village that the smugglers had their lair.

In Bawdsey Cliff the smugglers had a cave of no small dimensions. It had formerly been a hollow ravine in the earth, formed by the whirling of a stream of water, which had passed quickly through a gravelly bed, and met with opposition in this mass of clay. It had made for itself a large crater, and then had issued again at the same place, and ran through a sand-gall and gravelly passage down to the sea. This was discovered by a tenant of the Earl of Dysart, who in sinking a well near his shepherd's cottage suddenly struck into the opening of this cave. As the springs were low at this season, the cave was almost empty of water, and formed an archway into this curious place, and left it so for the gratification of public curiosity. Time swept on, and the cave became less frequented and at last was forgotten.

A few years, however, previously to the narration, some smugglers had been disappointed of their run, and had thrown their tubs down the well, with the consent of their agent the fisherman, probably a descendant of the old Shepherd's, who dwelt in the cottage. This led to the re-discovery and improvement of this famous depot of arms, ammunition, stock-in-trade, and place of retreat, which was then occupied by Will Laud and his associates, and to which very spot John Luff was at that time bound.

These men had continued to make the cave as comfortable a berth as a subterranean place could be. They had ingeniously tapped a land stream below the cave, and laid it perfectly dry, and with much labour and ingenuity had contrived to perforate clay into the very chimney of the cottage; so that a current of air passed through the archway directly up the chimney, and carried away the smoke, without the least suspicion being awakened. This place was furnished with tables, mats, stools, and every requisite for a place of retreat and rendezvous. The descent was by a bucket well-rope, which a sailor well knew how to handle; whilst the bucket itself served to convey provisions or goods of any kind.

It remains to relate that Bawdsey became the site of Radar Station Number One, commemorated by a plaque which records:

> In the year 1936 at Bawdsey Manor
>   Robert Watson-Watt
> And his team of scientists developed·
> The first air defence radar warning station.
> The results achieved by these pioneers played
> A vital part in the successful outcome of
>   The Battle of Britain in 1940.

This was unveiled by the Duchess of Gloucester in 1959. Curiously enough this work was done in a cave far deeper and larger than the one used by the smugglers.

The scene now moves across the water to Felixstowe Ferry, which must have been much the same as now, a pocket of littered buildings and shacks inhabited by an amphibious race. It has always been something outside our urban world, where artists linger, fishermen fish, boatmen mess about with boats. The outline of its huddle of houses against a blue or grey sky is balanced perfectly by the massive brickwork of the old Martello tower eastwards and, across the water, by the fringe of trees that line the distant scene. In reality, the Ferry is unique, geographically, nautically, and in the independence of its inhabitants. All they wish is to be left alone and live their lives in their own way. But it was from here, according to the tale, that the downfall of Margaret began, with a present sent by Will Laud now turned smuggler.

The narrative has just passed its deathbed scene, with the death of Margaret's sister Susan (Susan had warned Margaret against Laud):

> Poor Margaret and the family had returned from the funeral and were seated in the cottage, talking over the good qualities of their dear departed . . . and there came a rap on the door. . . .
> "Come in", said the father, and in walked a weather-beaten man, who from his dress might be taken for some honest ploughman, but whose countenance betrayed a very different expression. . . . His eyebrows half covered the sockets of his eyes, which

peeped from under them with an inquisitive glance, to see all was safe.

"Does one Margaret Catchpole live here?" said the man.

"Yes, she does," was Margaret's quick reply; "what do you want with her? I am she."

"Oh, you be she, do you? Then I be commissioned to deliver this here parcel into your hands;" and easing his shoulders of a heavy bale of goods they came with some weight upon the chair . . . vacated for the guest.

"From whom does this come?" said she.

"I don't know who he is. I was at work on the marshes at Bawdsey Ferry, when a young sailor came up to me, and asked me if I would take this here bundle to one Margaret Catchpole, a labourer's daughter, living as he described in just this place, which I have found."

"Did he give his name?"

"No; he said he couldn't come himself, but that this here would remind you of him."

The parcel was unpacked. There were silks and shawls, caps and lace, ribbons and stuffs, and gloves, parcels of tea, coffee, tobacco and snuff; together with curious-headed and silver-tipped pipes; in short enough to stock a small shop.

But the virtuous Margaret would have none of it and demanded the man to take the whole lot back. This he refused to do, particularly as he had had enough, walking the weary miles to Nacton carrying this impossible bundle on his back.

We might have a look at Nacton whilst we are there. It is still a most delightful spot and holds history as a comb honey. It was the birthplace of Sir Philip Bowes Vere Broke, of H.M.S. *Shannon*, and also the home of Admiral Edward Vernon, whom the sailors called 'Old Grog' from his coat and the fact he introduced grog into the Navy. Here, too, was Nacton Workhouse where there was a riot.

To the north of the parish, Alnesbourne Priory and Purdis Farm comprise some 777 acres. There were said to have been three churches, Hallowtree, St. Petronelle and Bixley. The name of the site was really Alvesbourn (Alve's burn, a brook that still runs into the Orwell). A large barn and farmhouse replaced the chapel and monastery buildings. A secret tunnel was said to run from the house to the Ancient House, Ipswich, home of the Sparrowe family,

Freston Tower

Butley Priory

Butchers Lane, Boxford

Mendlesham town armour

The guildhall at Laxfield

Lavenham

the entrance there being behind a panel in the chimney recess in one of the rooms. The barn is still at Nacton, but alas, the farmhouse was destroyed by fire only recently.

It was at this spot that Margaret's father worked as a farm labourer. It was famous for the production of barley, the best in the county. And it was here at the Priory Farm that the chapter on Harvest Home is based. Near what was Orwell station, on the Felixstowe line, are the Seven Hills of Nacton. These barrows are supposed to mark the spot where Earl Ulfketel engaged the Danes in 1010, rather than at Rushmere.

Levington, which adjoins Nacton, has an ancient church which sets the scene looking over Levington Creek and the Orwell. A lovely peaceful setting, so near the busy world yet quite beyond it. The upper part of the church tower and the almshouses were built by Sir Robert Hitcham whom we met at Framlingham.

That the 'Ship' is built of ships' timbers there can be no doubt, and that it was connected with smuggling there can be little doubt also; for under the thatched eaves is a cupboard. Here was the home of the Barrys and Margaret is alleged to have shown a lamp from here to guide approaching ships. That may well have been true for Levington is still a smuggler's venue to this very day.

And here, in passing, it might be mentioned was one of those long tenures in postal service. The Woolnoughs held that office since the Penny Post was first introduced in 1840; a service only recently broken.

Across the river is the famous Freston Tower, a folly built of red brick in the reign of Henry VIII. It has given its name to one of the novels by Richard Cobbold. It was designed by a William Latimer and built by Lord de Freston as a retreat for his daughter Ellen, and a place in which to study, using each floor in this order:

> The Lower Room to Charity from 7 to 8 o'clock.
> The second to working tapestry from 9 to 10.
> The third to music from 10 to noon.
> The fourth to painting from 12 to 1.
> The fifth to literature from 1 to 2.
> The sixth to astronomy at even.

How poor Ellen must have hated the place, although as it gives out on the river, she probably gazed on the lovely scene.

Nearby is the Cat House, which may have been built as a chapel. Naturally enough this figures in the Margaret Catchpole drama, as does old 'Robinson Crusoe of the Orwell'. He was Thomas Colson, who was hag-ridden and lived on a crazy craft of his own making that eventually sank in a storm, drowning him. He was the subject of one of Mrs. Cobbold's poems that appears in the *Suffolk Garland*. Colson also comes into the story on the side of John Barry, brother to Edward, who had also fallen in love with Margaret and stated his case on the assumption that Laud was dead. Robinson Crusoe was trying to sail up Orwell with a load of fish, past Woolverstone Park and the Cat House.

"The park boat was moored against the stair, and a single light burned against the window, at which a white cat might be seen to be sitting. It was a favourite cat of the gamekeeper's, which had accidently been killed in a rabbit trap, and being stuffed, was placed in the window of the cottage. Visible as it always was in the same place, in the broad day and in the clear moonlight, the sailors on the river always called that dwelling by the name of the Cat House; by which it is known at the present day."

One of the smuggling encounters when Laud was wounded takes place on the Felixstowe Ferry marshes, and the victim is taken to his father's cottage near the ruins of the old castle. Margaret visits him there: "Our travellers arrived at the lone cottage, where a faint, glimmering light from the low window told that the watch was still kept at the sick man's bed. . . ." A painful moan escaped his heaving chest, and at last he surprised the listeners by a sudden painful cry.

" 'Margaret, ahoy! Margaret, ahoy! Hullo! hullo! Don't run away. Here, here! I want you!' "

Plot succeeds plot. Laud is given out as dead, comes to life again, goes into the timber trade and gets mixed up with a gang of horse thieves. This leads to the *denouement* and Margaret's theft of her master's horse and famous ride to London dressed as a groom, followed by the inevitable hue and cry. How insignificant was Margaret and her supposed adventure is revealed in the fact that five lines announced the robbery in a newspaper report for 1797: "Margaret Catchpole, for stealing a coach horse, belonging to John Cobbold Esq., of Ipswich (with whom she formerly lived as a servant), which she rode from thence to London in about 10 hours, dressed in man's apparel, and having there offered it for sale was detected." (Incidentally, the horse was supposed to have been bought from Lord Rochford by Mr. Cobbold.)

Naturally enough Margaret is apprehended, brought to trial and condemned to death; is reprieved, escapes from prison, is recaptured, condemned to death for the second time; is again reprieved—owing, it is thought, to the powerful influence of the Cobbolds—and transported.

That Margaret Catchpole was a real person and Mrs. Cobbold a very kind woman is evidenced by the only tangible evidence that exists, in a letter preserved in the Christchurch Museum, Ipswich. Because, as Shorter remarks, "If Mr. Cobbold had an abundance of documents about this girl and her affairs, he must have destroyed them."

ipswich May 25, 1801.

honred madam

    i am sorry i have to inform you the Bad news that i am going away on wednesday next or thursday at the Longest so I hav taken the Liberty my good Ladey of trobling you with a few Lines as it will be the Larst time i ever shall trobell you in the sorrofoll Confinement my sorrows are very great to think i must Be Banished out of my owen Countrey and from all my Dearest friendes for ever it is very hard indeed for any one to think on it and much moor for me to enduer the hardship of it honred madam i should Be very happey to see you on tuesday Before I Leve englent if it is not to much trobbell for you for I am in grat confusion my self now my sorrowse are dobbled i must humble Beg on your Goodness to Consider me a Littel trifell of money it would Be a Great Comfort to your poor

unhappy servant

Margaret Catchpole.

6

The Villages of High Suffolk

How fine to view the Sun's departing ray
Fling back a lingering lovely after-day.

THE area described as High Suffolk, formerly known as the Wood-lands, extends roughly between Stowmarket and Harleston (Suffolk) and is virtually the centre of the county. It might also be described as the area of High Farming, because where the clay is tolerably uniform the land is often in a high state of cultivation. Producing the finest wheat in the kingdom, the area has small fields, low hedges and villages of colour-washed cottages of clay lump, an occasional thatched roof, set around a village green. There are over 100 villages in the area.

When Defoe made his tour of this part in 1772, it was full of rich feeding grounds and large farms employed in making the best butter and, in his opinion, the worst cheese in England; also in fattening great quantities of beef and mutton, turkeys, fowls and geese for the London market.

D. P. Dymond says that High Suffolk carried a population denser than anywhere else in England and vies with Essex for the greatest concentration of moated sites in the county. Moreover, the parish boundaries are much smaller than Breckland, and the road system so complex that sign-posts are of little avail. All in all, it is a very beautiful countryside, sheltered from the surging crowds, leading nowhere in particular, content in its own antiquity.

For the purpose of this division we will include the villages that lie between Ipswich and Stowmarket and begin with Bramford, pronounced as though it had got two or three *A*'s instead of one.

The outstanding feature of this village, threatened as it is by Ipswich, is the really noble church of St. Mary. This has a rare fourteenth-century stone screen of three arches, a sixteenth-century font cover with canopied sides and domed top and an alms box with the inscription—"Remember ye pore the scripture doth record what to them is geven is lent unto the Lord, 1591." The north-east buttress rests on a colossal glacial boulder. This delightful church has beautiful parapets on the north side and amongst the grotesques is a chained monkey.

Somersham church has a wooden south porch. Pegs fixed in the nave roof at the west end may have been for maidens' garlands. The gallows for the sacring bell still remains on the south side of the tie-beam above the altar rail.

The manor of Great Blakenham was given by Walter Gifford, in the time of William the Conqueror, to the abbey of Bec in Normandy. After the Dissolution of alien priories it was given to Eton College by Henry VI. The church of St. Mary, with a twelfth-century chancel, has a gem of a fifteenth-century wooden south porch with a figure of the Virgin in the gable niche.

Westerfield was of interest to those who travelled on the Yarmouth line, because of its little lamp-lit station, and the way in which the name was called out in broad Suffolk by the porters. The nice little church, which is almost visible from the station, has a fine single hammer beam roof that is continuous over nave and chancel. The village was always a great farming centre. In the old days the Swan Inn was kept by a blacksmith and there was a Swan's Nest Farm.

Barham is of considerable interest to me because that was my mother's maiden name. She was born at Middleton-cum-Fordley, and there is a Middleton Chapel in the church from a family of that name, which, of course, is pure coincidence. However, the Barhams of Suffolk must claim relationship with this village and its beautiful church.

Nettlestead, a quiet spot, has a Hall with an ancient gateway, on which are the quarterings of the Wentworth family. There is also High Hall, dating back to the time of Henry VIII. The church of St. Mary has a Tudor south porch and a very fine font. On the north wall of the sanctuary is a mid-seventeenth-century alabaster monument to Samuel Sayer and Thomasine his wife. John Blois was born here in 1560; he could read the Hebrew Bible when 6 years old and became one of the translators of the Authorized Version. Offton church has another of those wooden porches to the south door and a good tie-beam roof. The castle moat remains.

Great Bricett (Anglo-Saxon *brieseta*—settlers in a bright spot) lies in a valley, the surrounding plateau of which forms the watershed of south central Suffolk. It was once the seat of a Priory founded by Ralph Fitz-Brian and Emma his wife in 1110, for the Order of the Austin Canons, and was granted by Henry VI to the Provost and Fellows of King's College, Cambridge. West of the church of SS. Mary and Lawrence, which is set on the northern slopes and abuts on the one-time Manor House, is an ancient moated site known as Nunnery Mount or Nunnery Fields. This is supposed to mark the spot where the old priory stood. It consists of two flattened areas surrounded by water, forming in outline a rough figure of eight, and was, in all probability, the old fortress and bailey of the Norman owner of the manor.

The priory church is a peculiar little structure, with age-old rubble walls and a variety of windows. The beautiful fourteenth-century east window has been restored and glass of the four Evangelists now in the south window comes from it. The church nestles so close to the one-time manor house that its western door has no room to open. The recess of the archway is said to have been used as a wine cellar for the occupants of the house. Even the north door opens under a Tudor brick arch on to a garden. The jambs of the Norman south doorway have been repaired with inscribed stone, set sideways. Excavations carried out in 1926 revealed that the east end was formerly apsidal and there were two transeptal chapels, north and south, also apsidal. There is a particularly fine arcaded font and a most excellent tie-beam roof, besides good benches and bench ends.

Little Bricett is reached by crossing a humped-backed bridge, and is surrounded by a green with a row of cottages facing the church. Talmash Hall, attached to Offton, with its clustering chimneys was once occupied by the family of that name.

Ringshall has an extremely interesting little church which dates back to Norman times. Above the south door are some wall paintings depicting the Works of Mercy. There is a fourteenth-century roof to the nave and an excellent hammer beam roof to the chancel. The curious feature of the church is that the tie-beams go right through the walls and have huge wooden needles tying them in. The situation suggest a defensive position.

Once remote and peaceful, Great Bricett and Ringshall now have a large R.A.F. population and lie just a few hundred yards from what is reputed to be the noisiest runways in the country, used by squadrons of jet fighters based at Wattisham.

Both Baylham and Darmsden occupy charming positions above the Gipping valley with a view across the vale literally astonishing in such a county. Unfortunately it is marred by the ever-present pylons.

Shrubland Hall, really in Barham, home of Lord de Saumarez, is now a health clinic. The house, which is an Italianate Palladian building, stands high, but Sir Charles Barry's classical gardens have a splendour that ranks them amongst the finest in Suffolk. The view of the Gipping valley from the terrace is one that Constable delighted to paint, though it is now sadly obscured by wirescapes.

Coddenham is supposed to be the Combretonium of Antoninus. The Crown Inn, formerly 'The Gryfon', is thought to have been built about 1550 by a member of the family of Woodhouse, formerly owners of Crowfield Hall, for use as a dower house. The village had a body of archers who used the long meadow by the Pack road for assembly. The church of St. Mary is of a very early foundation. Within is a curious alabaster of the Crucifixion, with swooning Virgin and Angels with chalices, together with the Centurion. This was discovered in a house in the village believed to have formed part of the old monastery. It has been worked into a modern reredos.

Needham Market is almost in the centre of the county. Its name derives from the Anglo-Saxon for 'A home in need'. It has even passed into a Suffolk proverb: "You are in the highway to Needham", which Fuller elaborates thus: "Needham is a market town in this county, well stocked (if I mistake not) with poor people: though I believe this in no way did occasion the first denomination thereof. They are said to be in the highway to Needham who hasten to poverty."

The church of St. John Baptist has a marvellous double hammer-beam roof, one of the finest of the Suffolk timber roofs, which is saying something. Ingeniously constructed to bridge a wide span, it dates from the latter half of the fifteenth century and is quite unique. It is unique also in that the clerestory is made of wood. Up to late Victorian times, it was all cased in by a domed plaster ceiling, which at a restoration was removed and the roof exposed. It required a good deal of rebuilding.

Formerly all the pavements were of cobble-stones, carted from Battisford, and said to be the hardest in England. A square building at the corner of the lane leading to Barking church was known as 'Woodwards'. It was a grocer's shop so used since 1600 by that family. The last member died in 1923 aged 91, but the shop still carries on and belongs to the family.

And so we pass to Barking (Anglo-Saxon *berchingas*—dwellers by the birch trees), formerly the largest village in the Bosmere and Claydon hundred. Within a mile of Needham Market, it was once the mother parish. It delights in a most interesting church, with aisles, clerestoried nave and early chancel. Within, there is a pattern formed of grape-vines in relief about the windows, a good screen and parecloses. The old charcoal braziers are worthy of note, with their perforated lids and tripod stands on castors for easy movement. They are interesting survivals, although one must have been very close to them on a cold day to derive any benefit in so large a building. They flank a fourteenth-century chest of ample length. On the south wall is the old Serpent, which reminds one of the days when church music was thus made. It was played by Thomas Emsden in the church orchestra about 1830 and presented by his grandchildren. Barking is noted for its cedar trees.

At Barking Hall was found the beautiful bronze figure of a Roman Emperor, probably Nero (A.D. 54–68), with his left arm missing. It was presented to the British Museum by Lord Ashburnham in 1813.

Badley derives its name from the river Bat, which runs from Battisford to the Gipping, separating the parishes of Badley, Barking, Newton and Creeting St. Mary. Once upon a time a fine avenue of elm trees flanked Badley Walks, from the Hall to the main road, for nearly a mile. Tradition had it that it was a packway across the river to West Creeting church. The church away in the fields holds great charm with no modernization of any kind. The parish consists of not more than fifty souls.

Battisford had a preceptory of the Knights Templars of Jerusalem somewhere near the manor of St. John, north-west of the church. Sir Richard Gresham was the lord of practically all Battisford. His son Thomas built the Royal Exchange of Battisford oak during 1566. He died at his house in Bishopsgate on the 21st November 1579 and on the day of his funeral 100 men and 100 women of Battisford had black gowns costing 6s. 8d. the yard, given them in his will. There is said to have been a secret passage from the church to that of Badley.

Creeting St. Mary, Creeting St. Olaves and Creeting All Saints are three distinct parishes, ecclesiastically consolidated into one. St. Mary had an alien priory, a cell to Greston; and St. Olaves a cell to Bernay. Both of these were granted to Eton College, who also owned land in Newton in Creeting, as College Grove and College Grove Farm testify. Near Bosmere Hall a farm was formerly called Hungry Gut Hall, later known as Hungercut Hall. Dunch, a local family of very long standing, dating from the fourteenth century, left a charity which still exists. The church of Creeting St. Mary serves this rather scattered area.

Sally Woods Lane commemorates an old woman who lived in the remains of a cottage there. The tale runs thus:

Elizabeth Woods of Creeting Hills was born of respectable parents in 17– and now living in 1800, possessed on the death of her husband a life interest in 12 acres of land, with the house in which they lived, and of which she could never be induced to quit possession. The building, however, falling into decay was gradually demolished till nothing remained but the oven and two chimneys, in the larger of which this singular character and two daughters persisted to reside for sixteen years, with no further defence from the weather than a screen of bushes which they shifted according to the direction of the wind. A few boards composed their beds, the mother's head resting on a large flat stone, which was her seat by day, and her feet affording pillows to her daughters, whilst the oven served them as a wardrobe and store-room.

Creeting St. Peter or West Creeting has an extremely interesting little church with the remains of the best wall painting of St. Christopher in the county. It has an inscribed scroll: "Whoever looks at the picture of St. Christopher shall assuredly on that day be burdened with no weariness." Below is another fragment depicting a mermaid with a comb. The fifteenth-century pulpit is a heptagon.

There are three Stonhams which may be taken together. First Earl Stonham, the church of which contains the richest roof in existence, made of walnut. It appears to have been built on the site of a Roman crematorium. Stonham Parva has another fine church, with a hammer-beam roof. The Mouse brass, 1622, in the nave is both a memorial and a testament. Stonham Aspall church is noted for the wooden addition to the tower, which is situated on the south side forming a porch. This addition was made necessary because a young squire, an enthusiast in campanology, had the five bells recast with the addition of metal, into ten making it the first ring of ten in the county. Gosbeck has an early church, and amongst its treasures is an Elizabethan cup with the original tooled leather case inscribed: "Praises for God with honour and glory." An Act for burying in woolen" is kept in the safe. Crowfield Chapel has a wooden chancel. Nearby is a fine pigeon house dating from 1731.

Helmingham Hall is a quadrangular building of red brick diapered with black, and dates from the time of Henry VIII. It has the distinction of being completely moated, spanned by two bridges. These have drawbridges of wood next the house, one of which, the postern, is raised each evening. Mullioned windows and a fine oriel over the gatehouse, and its many gabled façades with their tall finials, set amid the sparkling water, presents a wonderful and romantic picture of the home of the Tollemaches. Its apparent newness (not so long ago it was stuccoed) and remarkably trim appearance are somewhat misleading. This is in part occasioned by the cleanliness of the water in the moat, for no weeds of any kind have been allowed to grow for many years. The Tollemaches are certainly the oldest family hereabouts and many soldiers, sailors and statesmen have been given to England in their distinguished sons.

Some of the noblest oaks in Suffolk are to be found in the surrounding parklands, as also some of the best examples of English furnishings within the walls of the house, which at one time possessed the original manuscript of Chaucer's *Canterbury Tales*. Here, too, was the lute made by John Rose on which Queen Elizabeth is said to have played. The gardens are very beautiful set amid four square brick pillars on which are winged horses' heads, the crest of the family. The country around was one of the haunts of the Great Bustard.

Helmingham Church of St. Mary, as one might expect, contains many monuments to the Tollemaches, some by Rysbrack and Nollekens. One of these is of such dimensions that a dormer has been thrown out of the nave roof to accommodate it, thus providing the church with a rather unusual feature.

Gipping possesses a most delightful little church that may have served as a private chapel to Sir James Tyrell. Local legend avers that it was built by Sir James in expiation of his part in the murder of the Princes in the Tower. According to the *Dictionary of National Biography*, before his execution for treason in 1502, he is said to have confessed to the murder. It is an extremely fine specimen of flush-work done in panels, monograms and rebuses, making a picturesque and beautiful little building. On the northeast buttress is the old French motto: *"Groyne que vodroy* (Let him complain who will)". The east window has remains of most interesting fifteenth-century glass, including the Tyrell crest—a peacock's tail in a boar's mouth.

Mendlesham is noted for at least two things: the wonderful

collection of town armour dating from 1470 to 1600, housed in a parvise over the north porch; and the creation of the Mendlesham Chair. The latter is something of great beauty and now of considerable value. It is a windsor type, where the legs and back are fastened into a solid hardwood seat, usually of elm. The frame is made of fruit woods, legs and backs, often inlaid with satinwood stringing. They were first made by Daniel Day, the local wheelwright, and then by his son Richard. Sheraton seems to have influenced the design.

But Mendlesham was the home of good craftsmen. John Turner was commissioned in 1630 to make a pulpit, font cover and reading desk. The two former remain and are worthy examples of fine work.

At Thwaite is a memorial to Orlando Whistlecraft, weather prophet and poet. Born in 1810, died 1893.

Gislingham has a most interesting church, with a double hammer-beam roof to the nave. The old box pews are retained, with a three-decker pulpit. But the chief item of interest is in the tower devoted to the ringers. Six are recorded of 1717, within an ornamental border. On a later board dated 1822 are others indicating the bells they rang, against badges of the trades they followed. One has a spade and coffin, he was the sexton; two and five an anvil for the blacksmith brothers Munn; three a bricklayer's trowel; four a hoe and six a shoemaker's awl, like the beak of an avocet. The Columbine Window in the church, painted by a fifteenth-century Flemish artist, is possibly the earliest known botanical record of the *Acquilegia vulgaris* in England.

Wetheringsett, a delightful village through which a tributary of the Dove runs quietly, had as it rector, Richard Hakluyt, who wrote in 1589 the *Principall Navigations, Voiages and Discoveries of the English Nation*. In the porch of the little church, which is surrounded by fine trees, is a short account of his life.

Aspall is one of the smallest parishes in England, but of considerable importance if we realize its implications. It is said to contain neither chapel nor pub. If the mother of a great sailor was born at Barsham, the mother of a considerable soldier was born here—Anne Frances Chevallier, whose son became Lord

Kitchener. He took as one of his titles that of "Aspall in the county of Suffolk". Although he was born in Ireland his father was a Suffolk man.

Aspall has been associated with the Chevalliers for many generations; they served its tiny church and tilled its fields to some purpose. One cultivated Chevallier barley which became famous; and another apples, in order that he might enjoy the drink he had been accustomed to in Jersey—and with the apples, mistletoe. To this end he had a granite cider press installed, the stone quarried on the coast of Normandy, shipped to Ipswich in the old hoys, dragged piece by piece over the old roads to its home in the cider house. It was working to within a few years ago. The first seed drill was used here in the last quarter of the eighteenth century. Arthur Young was a visitor and enthusiastic about what he saw.

Aspall Hall, a fine old mansion, is completely moated, standing on what is virtually a long oval island, the house built lengthwise, with a bridge over the water to the centre. Originally of lath and plaster, it was fronted with brick in 1702, during the occupancy of the Brookes. It is of considerable age and has jealously guarded all its ancient demesnes of stew ponds, moats and pigeon houses.

Worlingworth church has a very fine nave roof and a particularly good font cover, almost rivalling Ufford. The village is redolent of that strong clannish life which at one time so proudly existed. This is seen in the ornamental chains that suspend the canopy of the pulpit. These, with the delightfully finished wrought-iron crown, are the work of a local blacksmith. Then in the belfry, amongst the dust and the bats, was an old manual fire engine, and a huge oak beam that served as a spit as the inscription testifies: "An ox was roasted whole on this spit weighing fifty stones in this parish, given by the Rt. Hon. Lord Henniker, October 25, 1810. The day on which H.M. George III completed the 50th year of his reign." And again, "This beam was carried in procession to the Hall on the Jubilee of Her Glorious Majesty Queen Victoria and Empress of India on the 21 June, 1887. On which occasion the parishioners all attended Divine Service and afterwards all dined together, spending a most joyous day." It is recorded that when this spit was first used it was green and the sap oozing out tainted the meat.

Brundish church contains several good brasses, one being the earliest example in Suffolk of an ecclesiastic, 1360, Sire Edmound Brunnedissh in chasuble, over alb with apparels. Another is of John Colby, 1540, with Alice his wife.

Dennington church is thought to be on the site of a pagan shrine and possesses that rare survival, a hanging pyx. But it holds so many treasures, such as a dug-out chest, two parclose screens complete with lofts and staircases; and a sand-table for teaching the young idea how to write. The restored Bardolf tomb is splendid. The alabaster figures are of Sir William Phelip, Lord Bardolf and his lady. He was at Agincourt on St. Crispin's day and now lies here, with his wife on his right side, to show that his title came from her. He wears an SS collar.

The bench ends are a study in contrast to those at Fressingfield, cheek by jowl with box-pews. They are elaborately carved and stained to a mellow hue. In the centre aisle, south side, is a rarity in ecclesiastical symbolic carving of a Sciapus, the only one known in the country. The Sciapodes were a mythical race of giants, located in Libya, having but one webbed foot apiece. Pliny refers to them and says—"They have great power and pertinence in leaping." Here then he lies, in a Suffolk church, on his back, using his webbed foot as a sunshade, grasping under his arm two little headless dwarfs.

Badingham has a Seven Sacrament font, the panels of which are under rich canopies. It also has a fine hammer-beam roof. Once Badingham was famous for sheep, hence perhaps the beauty of the church.

Bedfield church has a most interesting font cover, described thus—"The lower stages are panelled. . . . For the administration of the sacrament, the three sides facing west detach completely and the three panels facing east hinge upwards and inwards, being caught up by a hook so that the sponsors may have a view of the ceremony."

On Saxtead Green is a first-class example of a Suffolk Post windmill. This has been restored and is kept as a show-piece of what our villages were like when these lovely creations were alive and twizzled in the wind.

Bedingfield church contains an ancient chest, 7 feet long, formed from a single log. There is a division inside across the middle with two lids 5 inches thick, sunk or rebated by means of cutting away the inner edge, thus forming a flange. This makes it almost airtight. Flemmings Hall was the home of the great family who gave their name to the village.

Denham, near Eye, has in the church the arms of Charles I, inscribed "16 C.R.37", and considered the best of the remaining examples of the period in the county. There is also a palimpsest Flemish brass to Anthony, third son of Sir Edward Bedingfield.

And so to Stradbroke, gleaming like a jewel amid the surrounding fields. The noble tower of the church dominates the huddle of houses. In the churchyard rests, after a wandering life, James Chambers, a queer itinerant ragged follower of the Muse, who, scorning comfort, wrote:

> This vile raiment hangs in tatters;
> No warm garment to defend:
> O'er my flesh the chill snow scatters;
> No snug hut!—no social friend!

He lies under an inscription to "the poor patient, wandering Suffolk poet".

Rishangles has a curious epitaph on a stone in front of the chancel steps, dated 1629, to two children, John and Alice Greene, who "lapwinge wise left the neast". What a charming valediction. Redlingfield's curious little church was that of a Benedictine nunnery. Athelington St. Peter has some wonderful bench ends with figures only 7½ inches high, one of which shows St. Margaret of Antioch with a book in her left hand, while she spears a dragon beneath her feet. She was evidently anxious to be fully employed. Wilby St. Mary is another fine church with an elaborate south porch and a richly carved Jacobean pulpit. Ubbeston St. Peter may have been built on the site of a Roman camp. The Tudor brick tower is said to be a duplicate of the ruined church of Linstead Magna.

Laxfield consists of a noble wide street with an unusually large church for so small a village. It has a memorial Baptist chapel to a local martyr, and a fine timbered guildhall with brick nogging. It also has the unenviable reputation of having produced William Dowsing, the despoiler of so many Suffolk churches. It is thought he may have spared his own, which has an excellent example of a Seven Sacrament font, in which he may have been christened. The church is screened by trees and hemmed in by the village inn and neighbouring buildings, but its glorious tower can be seen for many miles. Laxfield was once the terminus of the mid-Suffolk Light Railway and is High Suffolk at its best.

Heveningham Hall is built in the manner of the great Palladio, with its north façade consisting of pillars forming a portico. The wings are pedimented and the whole rests on rusticated arches. Sir Robert Taylor was the builder for Mr. Vanneck, a Dutch merchant settled in London, later to become Lord Huntingfield. This glorious achievement has just been purchased for the Nation at a cost of round about £300,000, the largest sum ever paid for the preservation of an historic building. Capability Brown laid out the grounds with serpentine paths and winding water, and planted groups of cedar trees.

Heveningham church has a good example of a Hall pew, and also the wooden effigy of a knight—Sir John Heveningham. He originally had a consort. They were both thrown out in 1847 to make fuel for a bonfire which consumed the lady, but the knight was rescued.

The decorated ceiling of Huntingfield church is the work of a Mrs. Holland, wife of a former rector, who laboured patiently under difficult circumstances. She was raised into position and left for hours at a stretch until the task was accomplished. On leaving the church take note of the old-world setting of the rectory, with its fragrant garden and the tall dark yew hedges that shut it in.

Cratfield church possesses the finest of the Seven Sacrament fonts, well-balanced, graceful and finely carved. It also possesses a clock concealed in a wooden cover, much like an old wagon. It is blacksmith made with gong and striking trains, and when about to strike there is a whirring and creaking suggestive of a local

A view across the pond at Polstead

Pargetting on a house at Clare

A carved bracket probably from the castle at Clare

Long Melford Hall

The moated Hall at Gedding

Gifford's Hall, Wickambrook

Cockfield: a house thought to have been a guildhall

ghost. Here, too, are a couple of ancient bookstands with chains. Wissett church has a particularly fine Norman north doorway, and a nice slender example of a round tower, with a splendid peal of bells. Metfield church has a fifteenth-century Brasyer bell, inscribed—"May this ring be blessed by the good offices of the Baptist."

Syleham church, set in the marshes of the Waveney, the approach to which is along an avenue of trees and through a five-barred gate, has a round tower. Its red-tiled cap shines in the sun and forms a distinctive feature as seen from nearby rising ground. A red-brick top has been added at a later date.

It was to Syleham that Henry II came to watch the preparations for the overthrow of Bungay Castle. In 1964 Colonel John Leader of Monks Hall in this parish paid a huge sum for an 11-acre farm that had originally belonged to the estate. He was determined to preserve this part of rural England. Monks Hall is one of the oldest inhabited buildings in England, dating back to 1450, and is officially recognized as a place of historic and national importance.

Fressingfield was once a woollen town and flourishing, and the old 'Fox and Goose' was the guildhall. The church presents an interesting study because it contains the most complete and best-preserved fifteenth-century bench ends of any in England. They consist of two sets mounted on a continuous plinth with ten ends to each aisle, thus giving forty in all, and only four of these are replacements. Beautifully cut trails run the whole length of the backs. One end of particular interest is that bearing "A.P." for Alice de la Pole, flanked by a cup and wafer. She was the granddaughter of Chaucer. Another shows St. Dorothea with her basket of roses.

Here is wood in the whole range of church history, tradition and doctrine, set out in a wealth of design and craftsmanship. But perhaps the most interesting thing of all is that the oak has been left to mellow, naturally bleaching, with a hammer-beam roof to match. This untouched oak has produced a wistful, silvery beauty which has to be seen to be believed.

Wingfield comes next and holds so much of interest, set in an ecclesiastical background, about which are two great names, those of Wingfield and de la Pole, the former uniting with the latter by marriage. Both families were of great consequence in the history of our land, powerful and influential, for the de la Poles were at one time within sight of, as almost within grasp of, the throne of England.

The family was founded by William atte Pool, a merchant of Hull, who not only created his family's fortunes, but that of Hull itself in the time of Edward I. His grandson Michael married Katherine Wingfield, of whose family the old couplet runs:

> Wynkefelde the Saxon held Honor and Fee
> Ere William the Norman came over the sea.

By her he entered into the estate here and made his home. He was created Earl of Suffolk in 1385. As the pages of history unfold, it was his grandson, another Michael, who fell at Agincourt, one of the only two English nobles to be spent on that field. It was his brother William who married Alicia Chaucer, widow of the Earl of Salisbury, who built the Suffolk church at Ewelme in Oxfordshire.

Wingfield Castle dates from 1384. Michael, Katherine's husband, obtained leave from the king to crenellate his house and to enclose and impark all the woods and lands belonging to the estate. It was dismantled about 1531 and the present farmhouse built by the Catelyns, tenants of Duke Charles Brandon. An ancient drawbridge, weighted by a huge stone, exists on the east side spanning the old moat which still surrounds the original plan. The main gateway is now the principal feature, and the original wall still exists within a few yards north-north-eastwards of this.

Wingfield church was collegiate to the adjoining College of Priests founded by Sir John Wingfield. Now a farmhouse, it is an interesting building, which possesses a couple of king-posts in the roof. Its peacefulness is reflected in the still waters of the fish pond at the rear.

Sir John lies under a canopied tomb in the chancel of the church, while on the other side of the priest's door is that of John de la Pole, second Duke of Suffolk, and his wife Elizabeth

Plantagenet; he is wearing the mantle of the Garter, and she the barbe or widow's plaited covering for the neck. They are carved in alabaster. Above are his tilting helmet with supporters. Another fine tomb is that of Michael de la Pole, Earl of Suffolk, and his wife Katherine Stafford; indeed the Stafford Knot is very much in evidence in the sanctuary. The effigies are carved in wood, and described as the "best in existence"; in their original colours they must have been very fine. In this spacious church, originally with a chapel of Our Lady, St. Margaret and another to the Holy Trinity, are stalls with misericords and parclose screens. Neither should one miss that peculiar little bit of woodwork, like to a sentry box, which was an eighteenth-century parson's shelter to enable him to conduct a funeral in comparative dryness.

From Wingfield we might run across to Hoxne and see Gold-brook Bridge, which crosses the Dove. Here the legend avers that King Edmund was detected hiding, given away by the glint of his golden spurs. His informers were two young people on their way to be married. As he was taken by the Danes, so it is said, he laid a curse on the bridge that it should never again be crossed by a happy bride. He was executed against a tree that became known as St. Edmund's Oak, and his body was covered with arrows like a porcupine with quills. When the oak fell in 1843, an arrow-head was found embedded in the trunk.

Not far removed is Brome, with its Hall, now modern, but then the home of the Cornwallis family, Knole-like in its splendour. It was always famous for the gardens and amazing collection of clipped yews and box trees. The family provided an apothegm—"There never was a Cornwallis a fool", while the Hall was accounted for in the couplet:

> Who built Brome Hall? Sir Thomas Cornwaleys.
> How did he build it? By the taking of Calys.

Some of their tombs are in the church, which has a round tower, the upper part of which was rebuilt in 1875.

Eye is said to have grown up around a fortified place, presumably the castle, of which the mound only remains. It was set for importance, for here was the chief Benedictine house of the county.

The great church of SS. Peter and Paul is a glorious fabric, with clerestoried chancel and nave, and aisles that run the whole length of the building. The rood screen is a grand affair surmounted by a richly carved triple cornice. In the lower panels are saints, including William of Norwich and Henry VI. There is a Jacobean cover to the font, and the fine Tudor brick porch covers an original carved door. But perchance you may know where the Red Book of Eye has got to. It was last heard of as being cut up for game labels at Brome! Eye also posseses a Suffolk peculiar in a crinkle-crankle wall, and a lovely example of a timber studded house near the church.

Yaxley has a rare survival in a Sexton's Wheel hanging over the south door of the church, which is also clerestoried and contains much of interest, including part of a fifteenth-century rood screen. Stuston, on the banks of the Waveney, has a round tower with an octagon top. Palgrave church is worth a visit, because of its lovely painted roof. The south porch has a parvise that contained the town armour.

Botesdale—Botolph's Dale—has no church but a chapel of the saint which joins on to a house, formerly a school endowed by Sir Nicholas Bacon, 1576. It was important in coaching days and has a pretty street. Botesdale Lodge has a Tudor wing dating from 1510, a seventeenth-century block about 1625, a bell cote put up in 1750 and a late Georgian block dating from 1816. This is just being brought back to life, after years of neglect, by a spirited owner, Mr. Grenville Powney.

Botesdale, Rickinghall Superior and Inferior adjoin, making one long street about a mile long. Of the two churches Inferior is the better with a round tower. Two seventeenth-century cottages in The Street, Rickinghall Superior, have just had a preservation order made on them as being of outstanding architectural and historic interest.

Burgate church has a magnificent brass on an altar tomb in the centre of the chancel. It is to William de Burgate, 1409, and Eleanor his wife. He is in armour of the camail period with a lion at his feet, she has a crespine head-dress and mantle. They are under a double canopy. Wortham church has the largest round tower in the county but in ruins. It is 29 feet in diameter with walls 4 feet thick.

The little thatched church of Thornham Parva contains a most extraordinary treasure in a retable of three sections, making 12 feet 6 inches in length. Each section has three panels divided from one another by slender pilasters with capitals, annulets and plinths, supporting Gothic arches. The figures are SS. Dominic, Katherine, John Baptist and Peter. The centre is twice the width of the others and shows Our Lord crucified, attended by the Blessed Virgin and St. John Evangelist. Then follows St. Paul, Edmund King and Martyr, Margaret of Antioch and Peter Martyr.

These paintings on gilt, with a background of gesso work, have been described as "in the very first rank of English art of the period" and date between 1300 and 1320. This is suggested by the primitive nature of the carpentry of the panels, for the arcades over the paintings have been cut from horizontal boards, pegged down on the vertical shafts, in exactly the same way as the mullions of early screens.

How the retable came to Thornham has been briefly told. Lord Henniker found the panels about 1926 in a loft in his stables. They came from Rookery Farm, Stradbroke, which in 1778 was bought with all its contents by one of his ancestors, Sir John Major, from a Catholic family named Fox, who had collected material to furnish a chapel.

Finningham has some bench ends in the church worthy of note. One has a woman's head appearing above a tower. Westhorpe was associated with Mary Tudor, Henry VIII's sister, who was married for the second time to Charles Brandon, Duke of Suffolk. He resided at the Manor House. Cotton church is mostly fourteenth century, with an angel roof and some noteworthy glass. The little thatched towerless church of Harleston has a Norman doorway. Shelland is chiefly remarkable because the church is dedicated to King Charles the Martyr. It is a donative and still has a barrel-organ in use. Great and Little Finborough might be taken as one. There is a beautiful view from Great Finborough churchyard, which adjoins the Hall, once home of the Pettiward family.

Haughley is thought to have been set for greatness, for it was a market town, but for some reason the lament arose: "Out of the ruins of Haughley, Stow arose." In the lower stages of the tower of St. Mary's, which serves as a porch, are thirty-three leather buckets suspended from the rafters and dating from 1725. It is recorded that the Abbot of Hales Abbey, Gloucestershire, to which this parish was appropriated, was ordered to erect a new pair of gallows in a field known as Luberlow. William Baxteyn was allowed the tenure of certain lands on condition he provided a ladder for use with the gallows. It would be of interest to know if more land was let on condition that the tenant provided a male-factor to test the means of execution. Haughley has the first ever picnic area in Suffolk, complete with toilets and opened in 1970.

Combs, or by its derivation Cambus (Anglo-Saxon *cambus*— 'on a long narrow ridge'), has a nice little church with a four-teenth-century wooden porch and a clerestoried nave, set away from anything that could be denominated a village. Presumably because it was adjacent to the Hall rather than the poor man's lodge. The Hall has gone but the church remains. The glass in the windows is exceptionally good, though it suffered damage in the guncotton mills explosion at Stowmarket. M. R. James describes the subjects: "In the south aisle window, the Works of Mercy, Ministering to the thirsty and Feeding the hungry. The story of St. Margaret, five scenes are left very much out of order. A geneaology of Christ."

On the uplands just south of the village is a farm called Holy-oak Farm, where lived a family named Kemball in the eighteenth century. Near the house is, or was, a venerable oak and tradition had it that a Bible was chained to this tree and at night folks assembled to hear it read.

Two miles north-east of Stowmarket, within the parish of Stow-upland, is another of those moated houses, so often met with in these parts, Columbyne Hall. This was evidently of very ancient foundation, thought to date from Danish times when invasion threats necessitated provision for menfolk and cattle to be with-drawn inside an unassailable enclosure, in this case provided by a wide and deep moat. Considerable interest attaches to the site by reason of an old illustration of the head of St. Edmund, set on a rayed background, with the inscription: "Head of St. Edmund. Formerly in the Abbey, Bury St. Edmunds. Beheaded by the Danish invaders Juga and Hubla at Eyberdun, now Hoxne in 870 A.D. at a great battle below Columbyne Hall in the valley of the Gipping."

7

West Suffolk

But soft! methinks I scent the morning air.   *Hamlet.*

I T is no mere caprice or accident that Suffolk is divided into the component parts of east and west, for they differ materially from one another, yet blend into a complete whole. Whereas the east has the sea-board and so many large rivers, with attendant marshy ground, the west has no waterways worthy the name, save the Lark in the north attended by the Linnet, and the Stour in the south which divides it from Essex. Nevertheless, the west has a loveliness all its own, and in many respects a greater claim to beauty. Bordering as it does on Essex and Cambridgeshire, it partakes in some degree of these counties, and nowhere rises to great heights. Pleasantly undulating, well wooded, with smiling fields that often run down to tiny streams such as the Brett, it shows every sign of a prosperous agriculture, forming at times wide-open spaces of great loveliness.

Like the east it has its contrasts—to wit, the sandling strip known as the Brecklands, ending, or shall we say, beginning, in the heathlands of Newmarket. Then, too, it holds a portion of that enigmatic strip known as the Icknield Way. Some have described this as "The war or battle road of the Iceni", running from Newmarket, crossing the Kennett at Kentford, and the Lark, ere it passes out of the county into Thetford. Also that Roman, or even earlier road, the Peddars Way, has been traced running up due south to north from Higham to Bardwell.

If the east was wholly given up to agriculture, nearly all the manufacture was carried on in the west. As the flocks battened on the sheepwalks of the eastern half, their fleeces were duly made up into Sudbury Bayes, kerseymeres or linsey-woolseys. Later there grew up at Lavenham a traffic in the horse-hair seating so much beloved by the Victorians as something that would last; and that of mats and matting at Hadleigh, household textiles at Haverhill, and silk weaving at Glemsford. Mention, too, must be made of that oldest industry of all, next to agriculture, flint flaking and knapping at Brandon.

And as a background to life, dynamic, colourful and upholding all, came agriculture. Out from that all else sprang, so that a servant in husbandry stood for a fine conception of life. Son followed father in ever-lengthening generations, ". . . and I require and charge Constance my wyff that she fynd my sonnys and daughters honestly in her power and yf she maye be departing owte of this worlds that my ii said sonnys, William Allen and John may heve some catayll and corne to sett up husbandry after her, and ever among us remember my soule with prayer".

The towns of West Suffolk are picturesque and full of interest, with their old winding ways. Hadleigh with its memoirs of martyrdom, manufactures and illustrious sons. Sudbury, redolent of Gainsborough, which Defoe described as "very Populous and very Poor". Bury St. Edmunds is deservedly the capital of this half, catching into itself memories of all the centuries, holding now but in a fragment what must have been the gem and lodestar of our bit of England, the abbey. Here all roads led, even across wild heaths, drawing all men's feet, including those of monarchy. On the other hand, Angel Hill is as good a piece of old township that one could wish to meet. Here, at the inn where Dickens slept, he caused Sam Weller and Job Trotter to meet, and here, for long enough, so great was his power of creation, Pickwick's ivory-handled knife and fork which he used were preserved. In fact they went with the house.

In the old days you could make the journey to Bury, via Sudbury and Long Melford, as did Mr. Pickwick, by the *Royal Mail, Red Rover, Times, Herald, Phenomenon, Old Angel, Cornwallis* or

Magnet. Starting the journey from 'Belle Sauvage', Ludgate Hill; 'Green Dragon', Bishopsgate; 'Blue Boar' or 'Bull', Aldgate; 'Golden Cross', Charing Cross; or the 'Flower Pot'', Bishopsgate Street. But you had to get up early for most seemed to leave about 5 a.m., although some were as late as a quarter before six, or six o'clock itself; while a few, evidently for the aged and infirm, left at noon. One can still hear the clatter of hooves on cobbles, watch the outside passengers holding tight as they swing out from under the archway of the inn yard. Even look with watering lips as one follows them into the cheerfulness of an old hostelry, such as the Sudbury 'Rose and Crown' or the Melford 'Bull', noting the frequent references to brandy and water, rum punch and other strong waters that seemed to disappear with the last coachman and the penultimate ostler.

Alternately, creaking wagons crept on through the night and sometimes through the day, headed as was but just and right by J. Bull, who made the adventure to Bury on Tuesdays, Thursdays and Saturdays from his namesake in Leadenhall Street. Mr. Hunt went from the 'Queen's Head', Borough; and Mr. Ruggle, as was fitting, from the 'Ipswich Arms', Cullum Street. Can you not see the dish of the old straked wheels, smell the sweat and delight in the curves and bulges of their old tilts, as they amble towards extinction? And above all, note how many of the drivers are fast asleep.

But these villages are a veritable harvest of harvests, a symphony of summers, as they are the fruition of a fine English tradition expressing honest purpose and nobility of conception. Since in this western half was the seat of manufactures and industry, centring about the woollen trade, there is more wealth evidenced and a certain amount of grandeur which the eastern half lacks.

As an introduction to the great Suffolk homes, it is of interest to quote from the *Household Book of Dame Alice de Bryen* of Acton Hall for 1412–13, published by the Suffolk Institute of Archaeology.

Taken together these accounts show the whole management of the household of a great Suffolk lady in the time of Agincourt.

The day-book gives in detail the numbers who were fed at her table, and exactly what they ate down to the last pigeon or herring. It gives a complete picture of the loaves, white and black, baked by the hundred at frequent intervals, and sometimes on a Sunday; how they were stored in the pantry; and how many were issued for each day's consumption. It shows the amount of malt used on each brewing day and records how much of the ale was drunk daily, and how the wine was brought into store in the pantry and issued thence. It shows the small purchases made day by day for the kitchen and how the horses of the household and the guests were fed and bedded. It records the arrival of the fishmonger, and enters the date at which each cade of herrings was begun. The lady not only took her meals with the household and her guests, she also demanded a strict account of all that they ate. . . .

The purchases are of all kinds. They include payment for grain and cattle, fish, salt and spices, for the home manufacture of candles and tapers out of the kitchen fat, for the repairs of buildings, for labourers employed in mowing the lady's meadow, and watchmen preventing the theft of her hay, for the shoeing of her horses, for kitchen utensils carefully recorded down to the earthenware pans for catching dripping, the strainer price 2d. the pestle also priced 2d. and for sharpening of the kitchen knife.

The churches in many respects rival those of the eastern half. Those of Lavenham and Long Melford are almost unsurpassable in their beauty and grandeur, so near to one another and yet so different in detail.

The literary associations of West Suffolk are strong and definite, beginning with Jocelin, the Boswell of the famous Abbot Samson. He was discovered by John Gage Rokewood, before Carlyle made him into a popular character. Rokewood had the original Latin text published by the Camden Society, and it was this edition that Carlyle used.

Next in order comes Lydgate, some two centuries later; he was also an inmate of the famous abbey. He was associated with Caxton and became a disciple of Chaucer, to whom he submitted some of his manuscripts.

Sir Thomas Hanmer, the first editor of Shakespeare, was educated at the famous Bury Grammar School. He lived for long at the manor house, north of Mildenhall church, much the sort of life associated with the celebrated Sir Roger de Coverley. Arthur

Young, the famous agriculturist, although born at Whitehall, 11th September 1741, was the son of the rector of Bradfield and educated at Lavenham. Thomas Tusser pursued his calling in Suffolk, but was born in Essex.

The late Claude Morley claimed another Dane Stone, similar to that at Halesworth, in the church of St. Michael, Hunston. This church was burnt down some years ago—it was thought by Suffragettes—and has been rebuilt. Two of the market crosses remaining in the county are in this half, one at Lavenham the other at Mildenhall. They vary greatly in character. The other example is at Bungay. Of the round towers, only four, those of Saxham Parva, Risby, Hengrave and Beyton are in this half.

8

The Villages of West Suffolk

Fen yellow-bellies;
Cambridgeshire dumplings; Suffolk asses;
Essex calves; Hertfordshire hedgehogs.

STARTING from the south we come to Nayland on the Stour.
The church has the distinction of an altar-piece by Constable—
"Christ blessing the Wine at the Last Supper". There are also
some panels of a screen and a memorial to the Reverend William
Jones, who was perpetual curate, dying in 1800. A new spire to
replace one that fell in 1832 has been recently erected. This is a
very beautiful and retired spot.

And so to Wissington with which it is associated. The little
Norman church possesses much of great interest in the nave arch,
beautiful south doorway and lovely font. The village is tucked
away in peace, surrounded by old Tudor cottages, and its wooden
bell-cote sticks up amid the trees.

Bures St. Mary on the banks of the Stour is another church
with interesting details. It has a wooden north porch, and a
south porch of sixteenth-century brickwork. There is too an
excellent armorial font. The monuments include a wooden effigy
of a Cornard, crossed legged. He was alleged to have sold the
farm called Corn Hall for 4d. in the reign of Henry III. A bridge
across the river connects it with Halstead.

Stoke by Nayland church dominates the landscape; the tower
can be seen from Harwich. The south door, 10 feet 6 inches high,
is carved with the Jesse-tree, and the armorial font stands on

three high steps. The church is cathedral-like in its proportions and contains many memorials to the Howards, Tendrings and Rowleys. There is also a Mannock chapel, and a fine brass to Sir William Tendring, dated 1408.

Gifford's Hall, with its notable gateway, flanked by two octagon towers of red brick, bearing the Mannock arms, is one of Suffolk's great houses, dating from the time of Henry VI. It stands amid wooded surroundings and is approached by a long and pleasant drive. This is really a remarkable house, built round a court, with gatehouse, hall and minstrels' gallery. It was in the Mannock family for 300 years. There is another Gifford's Hall at Wickham-brook.

Polstead is noted for at least three things: cherries, a four-teenth-century tower to the church with the original stone spire, and a melodrama of the Red Barn mystery. The village itself is in a lovely position, set in undulating pasture land, with a mere near the church that adds no small feature to the landscape. Polstead 'Blacks' are still available.

The main entrance to the church is by the north porch. The nave retaining its twelfth-century arcades with brick arches is unique. Once this church had a Norman western façade, which has been obscured by the tower, and inside the latter is a fine Norman doorway. Amongst its treasures is the original paper register dating from 1538, the first year that registers were ordered to be kept.

West of the Church are the remains of the Gospel Oak, around which services were held a thousand years ago. And so to this day, on the first Sunday in August, although now it is around a sap-ling grown from an acorn of the old tree.

Assington St. Edmund is situated in parklands adjacent to the Hall, and the south doors are amongst the best in the county. They are richly traceried and surrounded by a carved trail of birds and vines. It is reputed to have been built by Cnut the Great on the field of the last battle fought by him.

Newton, near Sudbury, has in the church two things of great interest, notably the early fourteenth-century piscina and sedilia formed by four arches and detached pillars. But the chief feature is the beautiful tomb in the north wall of the chancel. It is thought to be that of Margaret Boteler, 1310, an altar tomb with an effigy in a recess richly canopied over. The village also possesses a green of about 60 acres.

Boxford (Anglo-Saxon *box-ford*, 'a ford by the box tree'), a happy village, "situated in a bottom between two brooks". It consists of old houses, shops and crofts surrounding a fine old church, with a mill and a proprietary stream, the Box. This is but another of the old woollen towns, of greater renown than some of its neighbours. Here in 1524 were employed sixty of the inhabitants in the industry, against fifty-seven at Lavenham, twenty-eight at Melford and twenty-seven at Sudbury.

The church of St. Mary, dating from the fourteenth and fifteenth centuries, is notable for its contrasting porches, that on the north being of wood, that of the south, unusually, of stone. The south porch shows that much thought went to its building, for it is mentioned in wills as early as 1441. It covers a fine door. The font cover is an interesting example of seventeenth-century workmanship, and when open reveals painted scrolls on which are texts from John III, 4.5.18.

In the chapel of Our Lady are traces of wall paintings of Edward the Confessor, complete with ring and sceptre; while above is a kneeling figure on a fald stool. But this is not all, for there is a memorial worthy of attention:

> In Memory of Elizabeth Hyam of this Parish
> for the fourth time Widow, who by a Fall
> that brought on a Mortification was at
> last hastened to her End on the 4th. May
> 1745, in her 113th year. ✓

And there is a small brass to David, son of Joseph Birds, 1606, aged 22 weeks. It is in the south chancel aisle, portraying him in his cot. There is another to "William Doggett, 1610, aet 53, Marchant adventurer, citizen and mercer of London, and free of the East Indian Company". It is not clear if this is the same family as that who provided the Doggett Coat and Badge for the Watermen's Derby, and the City's oldest boat race.

Groton must be mentioned for a great name, that of John Winthrop, born here in 1588. He was the first Governor of the Massachusetts Bay Colony, where so many East Anglian names can be found. A window in the church has been placed to his memory.

There is always something unusual to be discovered in a Suffolk church, if you know where to look for it. For example at Edwardstone is a brass to Benjamin and Elizabeth Brand, 1620, recording that their twelve children were "all nursed with her unborrowed milk".

Chilton Hall is an old stuccoed building, situated between the Waldingfield High Road and Chilton church. The entrance is by a bridge over the moat that surrounds the Hall and grounds. Somewhere near is a barrow. The church, with its brick western tower, has some Crane monuments. One with a single figure, the other with a man wearing an SS collar, and his wife.

Acton was responsible for that wonderful household account we have previously quoted, remembering it is but a village. It is not surprising that the church contains two fine brasses. One is to Sir Robert de Bures, 1302. This brass is the third in the country in point of age but takes precedence on account of its preservation, being perfect, while the others are defective. Boutell says it is the finest military brass in existence. The other is to Alyce de Bryan, kinswoman of Sir Robert de Bures and the lady of the accounts.

And so we come to Long Melford, with which few, if any, of the Suffolk villages can compare in interest. Well named from its long broad way that runs past the homesteads and shops of varying ages, alongside the green and out to Bury. The name actually derives from Mel, a mill, one of the Domesday mills, and a ford over a little stream, the Chad, which rambles on to join the Stour. Today one crosses the ford by a bridge and is reminded of all the little river stood for in the ancient brick conduit on the green.

To possess such architectural features as Melford Hall, Kentwell Hall, Melford Place, and the incomparable church, to say nothing of the hospital within its enclosures of red brick, in one

The Priory, Stoke by Nayland

Long Melford Church

Kersey: *(left)* the sign of the Mare's Tail, *(below)* a street in the village

(above) The pack-horse bridge at Moulton

(below) A gypsy's grave by the side of the A45 near Moulton

(above) Gazeley Mill

(below) Pakenham Mill

community, is to suggest a concentration of excellence hard to equal.

Through the long years this has been the patrimony of the great and the discerning. For it was to a Melford Hall the abbots of Bury came in retreat and excursion, to a house that existed on the site of the present building. The renowned Abbot Samson often lived here from 1182 to 1211, to enjoy by observation, rural sports and occupation: "He did not honte himself and he favoured not that his monks shoulde, but he lyked much to sytte in a stylle place in ye Melford woodes and to see ye Abbey dogges honte ye stagges." Suffice to say the St. Edmund's breed of hounds was famous in those far-off days, as also their sheep. And it was to this abbot that Melford owed its markets and its fair, originally granted by King John and confirmed by Henry II.

At the Dissolution the Hall, in common with the other wealth of the abbey, became vested in the Crown. Subsequently it was granted by Henry VIII to Sir William Cordell, Kt., a Melford man who became Master of the Rolls to Queen Mary, and Speaker of the House of Commons to both Mary and Elizabeth. It was he who built the magnificent and essentially English Tudor house that still stands, making for himself a home and a lasting memorial. So well did he build that Elizabeth was pleased to visit her minister's new home, surely a memorable occasion. The window in which she appears in characteristic dress, placed in her honour, still survives.

The house itself is of red brick, probably made in the village, for the pond on the green is known as the Claypit. It is of the traditional E-plan, and was originally moated; evidence that it was built on the site of an earlier building is to be seen in the vaultings of the cellars, dating from medieval times. The chief features are the six towers, rising from square bases, turning to octagon turrets, capped by leaded cupolas, in which the fan-shaped motif over the porch is repeated. The cupolas taper into nothingness and fulfil the fine aspirations of the Tudor builders, breaking the sky-line, carrying light and grace to what might have been a heavy mass. The chimneys have survived with their finely moulded caps and bases; the rain-water heads are ornamental and inscribed with the cockatrice badge of the Cordells. The whole is wrought in the splendid tradition of the great East Anglian builders, whose brick masterpieces have happily survived from the earliest days of the thirteenth century.

A good deal of alteration took place in Georgian times. The building was completely re-fenestrated, the stone mullions removed and sash windows inserted. The interior came in for attention, the hall was remodelled, the rooms replanned and new fireplaces inserted. The gatehouse was removed and the square forecourt was replaced with the present semi-circular sweep.

For long there existed an ancient wooden porch of uncertain date. It had a high-pitched roof supported by grotesque figures in costume, typical of the Henry VII period.

Yet another gem of Melford is to be found at the end of an avenue of lime trees that sweep in a curving mile from the line of the church to the red-brick moated Hall of Kentwell. This house was for long associated with the Cloptons, who were responsible for the magnificent church, and was probably built by Thomas Clopton, who died 1597.

Like Melford Hall it is E-shaped, of old red brick, but retains its mullioned windows, and has been but little altered since it was built. Although there was a fire in 1826, when the dining-room was destroyed and the devastation extended through to the garden side. Happily, it still retains its moat, and the reflection of wall and chimney, cupola and dormer, are mirrored in the placid water-lilied depths. Two bridges span the small divide, west and south, leading to the creeper-hung and lichened walls, while yet another moat encloses the gardens. A record made in 1676 describes it as "a very fair brick house, with twelve wains-cot rooms, and other conveniences, besides timber in the grounds and wood considerable".

The property passed by sale to Sir John Robinson, Protonotary of the Common Pleas in the time of Charles II. Early in the eighteenth century it was again sold to John Moor, and passed from his family to Robert Hart Logan, High Sheriff of the county in 1828 and M.P. for the Western Division. In 1838 it was again disposed of, this time to the Starkie Bence family. As I write

(1970) it has again been sold with 2,750 acres of land, owing to the death of Mr. C. D. B. Starkie Bence.

It is hardly to be wondered that so glorious a cluster as Long Melford constitutes should be crowned with a magnificent and unique church. This dates from the fifteenth century, when it was rebuilt by subscription of the wealthy local families, those of Clopton, Martyn, Dister, Hill, Ellis and Harset. The chancel came first, about 1479, the nave in 1481, followed by the south aisle, porch and Martyn chapels in 1484, with the Lady Chapel in 1496.

The distinguishing and unique feature is the external inscription that runs the whole length of the sides, including those of the Lady Chapel. The lower inscriptions are cut deep in blocks of stone, the letters being about 8 inches high. The upper inscriptions are stone letters of a larger size, embedded in the mortar, faced with small flints.

There is a good south porch and a brick tower with pinnacles at the angles. This is modern and replaces an eighteenth-century monstrosity that had been erected when the first and more worthy specimen was destroyed by lightning. In falling, it carried away part of the inscription.

The nave has a good flattened tie-beam roof, and there is no chancel arch to break the view. The richest gem is the Clopton Chantry, a really beautiful enclosure on the north side of the altar. In his will, 1494, John Clopton directed that his body should be buried in the "lytell chapell in Melforde Churche, there my grave is reddy made, even by my wif". Above are twelve canopied niches, evidently intended for statues of the Apostles, and under these are shields, bearing the arms of the Cloptons, impaling their alliances. The roof is extremely interesting, painted blue with applied gilt stars, and decorated with carved foliage and broad labels, bearing black-letter inscriptions. Those decorating the carved cornice or wall-plates are taken from a religious poem by Lydgate, the monk of Bury.

The church once had a goodly array of brasses, but most have gone. It also shone with colour through its hundred windows. Time has dealt hardly with these, but some remains have been collected into the chancel windows. An interesting fragment has been noted, dating from the fifteenth century, containing three rabbits, each with two ears, yet there are only three ears for the lot. This is thought to be a novel representation of the Holy Trinity. Another rarity is in the window over the north door, known as a Lily Crucifixion. Our Lord is shown hanging from the stem of the lilies as emblems of purity, nailed to petals, and no cross appears. The hands are nailed to flowers and the right foot is placed over the left, while a single nail pierces both.

Another rare treasure is the sculpture in alabaster, gilded and coloured, of the Magi. This was found in the floor of the church, probably placed there by 'Masr Clopton' in the days of Edward VI, against the hope of happier times, that it might emerge a symbol of his father's faith.

The most interesting feature, appearing externally as a triple-roofed chancel, is the Lady Chapel at the east end. This magnificent little entity has an ambulatory, divided off with three arches north and south, bearing canopied niches at the angles. It has a similar timbered roof to the Clopton Chantry. For a century and a half this lovely building was used as the village school, witness the multiplication table in a panel on the eastern wall. Afterwards, for a space, it was a lumber room. It is now happily restored to its original intention. Note also the Coaching Inn or Act of Parliament Clock, in japanned case, by Thomas Moor of Ipswich. This is reminiscent of the old clocks, the figures IIII, V and VI of which were completely worn away by the fingers of carriers and drovers feeling for the time in the early mornings in days before a match.

Holy Trinity Church, which attracts about 10,000 visitors a year, is in the process of being extensively repaired by a fund that was launched by Benjamin Britten some years ago.

A mile or two further north is Stanningfield, which holds in its deep recesses Coldham Hall, dating from 1574. It was built by a Rokewood, one of whom, Ambrose, was executed at Tyburn in 1605 for his part in the Gunpowder Plot.

The Rokewoods, who originated at Acton, appear an unfortunate lot. Two sons fell in support of Charles I, Robert at Oxford,

William at Arlesford. Another, Ambrose, a brigadier-general in James II's Guards, was executed at Tyburn in 1696 for his part in the treason known as the Barclay Conspiracy. An earlier Roke-wood, who attempted to entertain Elizabeth I in her famous passage through Suffolk, was flung into prison at Bury by her, where he died. His offence being that he was a Catholic. The family became extinguished on the male side and, through a daughter, was merged into the Gages of Hengrave. The latter is thought to have given the name to the greengage plum.

Coldham Hall was built by Robert, whose initials appear over the porch. It is of the traditional *H*-plan, and was originally moated. In the south-west corner of the garden is the finest dove-cote in the county. Built of red brick, with white brick dressings to window openings and corbel tabling, it is raised on a battered plinth. The roof is conical, covered with old English tiles, mellowed with age, and crowned with a cupola standing on six legs, bearing a circular cornice and hemispherical dome with a knob pinnacle.

Cavendish possesses a really noble church, with old-world thatched cottages that nestle beneath its shadow and around the Green, thus presenting a picture that has almost become a Suffolk show-piece. The name, according to Skeat, derives from 'Cafa's Eddish' (meadow), Cafa being the owner's name, and eddish a word in use a few years ago, meaning aftermath, or second crop. From here sprang the great family of the Dukes of Devon-shire.

In the church is a fine and unusual lectern of wood, with chains attached to Jewel's *Apology* and the *Book of Homilies*. There is also a sixteenth-century brass lectern, said to have been given by Elizabeth I.

And so to the Honor of Clare (Anglo-Saxon *Clara*—possibly Clara's place). A delightsome little market town with open, clean, spacious streets and fascinating houses, many with gardens that run quietly to the Stour. Here again is so much of history, centring about the castle, built in all probability by Norman Gilbert de Clare, afterwards Earl of Hertford. This ancient monument, which figures in the Domesday Survey and dates from Saxon times, stands at the juncture of the Chiltern river with the Stour. All that remains are the earthworks, 53 feet high, and a buttressed fragment of the Keep.

Lady Elizabeth de Burgh, who figures much in Clare history, and who founded Clare College, Cambridge, sometimes lived here. And somewhere amid the few remaining ruins she housed her immense retinue of 250 persons, which was large enough to include a marshal's department, and several hundred horses. Amongst the amenities was a vineyard, also mentioned in Domesday, the grapes of which may have given the name to claret.

The Swan Inn bears a magnificent carved bracket, 10 feet long, formerly a window sill. An aged inhabitant living in 1850 remembered it being in position as such, although it probably originated from the castle. In the centre is a white swan, gorged with a crown and chained to a tree on the left, from which depends two suns. It has been surmised that it may have been executed in the reign of Henry IV, between 1399 and 1413.

Clare was another of the woollen towns, and it is thought that the 'Bear and Crown' was the old wool hall. Before it stood the market cross, which was demolished in 1839. The woollen trade became extinct about 1825, by the death of the last weaver aged 83. Straw-plait for ladies' bonnets was made here in the days of cottage industries.

The Honor of Clare and the lordship passed from the de Clares to the de Burghs, and from thence to the Mortimers and so on to Edward IV, who gave them to his mother, Cicely of York. Surely it is of significance that this small, but delightful, place has given its name, not merely to earls, but to County Clare, the Dukedom of Clarence, Clarencieux king of Arms, and Clare College, Cambridge. Added to which is Claremont, Esher, a one-time royal residence; the Deanery of Clare; Clare Market in London; and an estate in Essex belonging to the Dean and Chapter of St. Paul's, Clare Downs.

The church is fine, consisting of a clerestoried nave and chancel, with north and south aisles, and a south porch. Some portion of the screen remains in the south aisle, and there is a sixteenth-century eagle lectern as at Cavendish. There is also a huge sepulchral slab that covers Robert de Godewyk, Prior Provincial of the Augustine Order in England. The Barker pew is an interesting survival, complete with sconces, raised on stilts above the south doorway. There is also a Ringer's Gotch of 1729. This was carried in procession, the ringers soliciting for it to be filled. When it reached its hundredth birthday, the landlord of the Bell Inn filled it for the ringers, who used his house as a centre for their meetings.

Adjoining the churchyard is a fine specimen of Suffolk pargetting, the most elaborate of its kind, on the side of a fifteenth-century house. Dated 1473, it consists of conventionalized flowers, standing out in good relief, divided into panels. These cover the overhangs of the gable and the side wall facing the churchyard. In the western gable is a shield bearing the Arms of the Earls of Clare, three chevrons. At the south end of the township is another house so decorated, with large rectangular panels, roughcast, and surrounded by a repeating pattern.

The Priory, now a lovely house embowered in trees, is a perfect example of adaptation, so often met with in this county, from an ecclesiastical purpose to a domestic dwelling, preserving the more easily convertible portions, such as the walls of the cloister garth, a few odd portions of the dorter and frater, the infirmary, and the offices and prior's lodging which form the house itself. These were reconstructed after a fire which swept the place in the late fifteenth century. The ceiling of the present hall is thought to date from that period. This is one of several in Clare, all bearing a strong family resemblance in carved trails along a central beam, with radiating and stopped rafters. The best of these, that from Church Farm, has been removed to the Victoria and Albert Museum.

The most interesting feature of the priory is the lobby forming the entrance, with its decorated window and unique star-fish vaulting. The finely moulded hall door of oak is similar in character to the two fourteenth-century doors of the church. Here is the burial place of the first Duke of Clarence, of whom Fuller remarks: "Happy had he been, if either nearer to it [the throne], so as to enjoy the honour thereof, or further off, so as not to be

envied and suspected for his title thereunto by king Henry the
Fourth."   King Edward the Third's son was he,
                  Sir Lionel, which buried is hereby;
                  And for such a prince too simply.

Nethergate House is one of note, which for long was occupied
by the Crosse family, wool merchants and cloth workers, who
brought much prosperity to the town in their day. It is a
Tudor house, but the chimneys are not original. A Miss Jefferies
of the Ipswich engineering firm lived here, and it was she who
carried out the extensive alterations, including the chimneys and
the wing on the left. These were so cleverly done by a Mr. Turner
as to be taken for originals. The garden was probably the taynter's
yard where the cloth was stretched, and ran back to the river. Sir
John Hope, the great antiquary, succeeded Miss Jefferies in the house.

Under a shop in the square is a remarkable undercroft
chapel, 20 feet square. This has a central octagonal pillar and eight
semi-circular pilasters rising from the floor, dating from about
1490. This may have been a Morrow Mass Chapel. The Cliftons
is also a notable house; and the old Maltings retain their beautiful
Suffolk building characteristics.

Walter Lorking, a poor lad of Clare, employed in digging in the
Castle Bailey in 1865, had the extraordinary luck of turning up
an extremely precious reliquary, consisting of a gold crucifix
attached to about 2 feet of chain, all of exquisite workmanship.
The cross 1½ inches long, studded with a large pearl at each
intersection of the upright and transverse pieces. A small pin
fastens a portion of the upper side of the cross, which can be
removed. Inside is a small piece of wood and a minute fragment
of granite. There is a good deal of evidence to support the belief
that this formed part of the jewels belonging to Edward III.

The discovery was made known to Queen Victoria's Treasury,
whereupon Her Majesty notified her desire to possess the relic.
She was pleased to reward the finder with three golden sovereigns.
So after 500 years it again passed into Royal ownership. I understand it is now in the British Museum. Clare Castle and environ-
ments is likely to be one of the first of the country parks.

From here it is but a short way to Stoke by Clare, another pretty village. The church is tucked away in the park, near a dovehouse, or something of the kind. Early in 1948 wall paintings were found of which some are thought to be the last executed in an English church before the Reformation. The pulpit is considered to be the smallest in the county, with a diameter of only $20\frac{3}{4}$ inches. It is an excellent piece of craftsmanship. Note, too, the chest on which the iron-work breaks into lively branches. The medieval clock bell is inscribed, "Rise in the morning to serve God".

Kedington, pronounced 'Ketton', was the home of one of Suffolk's most ancient families, the Barnardistons. Sacheverall Sitwell, in his introduction to Mrs. Esdaile's book, reminds us that at one time they were the most important family in the county, who can be traced back to a time when surnames were not yet hereditary, and who flourished for twenty-seven generations in a direct line. Neither should it be forgotten that it was a Barnardiston who caused Queen Henrietta to exclaim when she observed him, "See what a handsome Roundhead is there!"

Their pew is in the delightfully furnished and characteristic Suffolk church, which stands heavily screened by trees, sometimes called the Westminster Abbey of Suffolk. The whole scheme, including the ancient benches and the memorials, constitute a happy and rare survival, probably unique in the country. On the apex of the chancel gable is a Saxon crucifix, dating from A.D. 900, which may have formed part of a Wayside Cross. It is said to have been unearthed A.D. 700, and represents Our Lord as a child, the Youthful Victor. The way to the old Hall, now demolished, is marked by the avenue of trees, planted slantwise across the north side of the churchyard.

The Barnardiston memorials, effigies and hatchments, adorn the church, with the beautiful crest of a heron or bittern standing in a bed of reeds, as we saw at Brightwell. The kneeling effigy of a young girl is particularly fine.

Withersfield church is noted for some remarkable poppy heads to the nave bench-ends. One is of St. Michael weighing souls and another shows St. George slaying the dragon. Poslingford has an interesting Norman doorway and some wall paintings. A farmhouse, once owned by the Right Honourable W. H. Smith, of newspaper and book fame, had relics of Chipley Abbey, an Austin priory annexed to Stoke College. Great Thurlow, on the borders of Cambridgeshire, gave its name to that family. In the church is a very fine brass of a man in armour, with wife in veil headdress, dated about 1460. Great and Little Bradley continue the line to the Cambridge border. The church of the former possesses one of the earliest bells in Suffolk and has a Norman doorway.

Little Bradley has a round tower and is really a small Norman church. Here is a brass to John Daye, 1584, who printed Fox's Book of Martyrs. He was born at Dunwich and the first English printer to use the Saxon type. He printed the works of Parker, Latimer and Fox and was imprisoned during the reign of Mary. When the Company of Stationers obtained their charter from Philip and Mary, he was the first person admitted to the livery, and in 1580 was Master of the Company, to which he bequeathed property at his death. His name is perpetuated today by the John Day Publishing Company of New York.

> Here lyes the Daye that darkness could not blynd,
> When Popish fogges had overcast the sunne;
> This Daye the cruel night did leave behind,
> To view and show what bloodie Actes were donne.
> He set a Fox to write how Martyrs runne
> By death to lyfe. Fox ventured paynes and health;
> To give them light, Daye spent in print his wealth,
> But God with gayne returned his wealth agayne,
> And gave to him as he gave to the poore.
> Two wyves he had partakers of his payne:
> Each wyfe twelve babes, and each of them one more,
> Als was the last increaser of his store;
> Who, mourning long for being left alone,
> Sett upp this tombe, herself turned to a stone.

Stradishall is noted as being the village in which Thomson the poet wrote the "Winter" of his *Seasons*. And the rectory is noted because many of the screen panels and parts of the Holy Table have been used in framing the windows.

Cowlinge once had two fairs, one for cattle and sheep on 31st

July and another on 17th October. The church has a brick tower and two brasses, one to Robert Heigham, 1571 aged 45, the other to Thomas Dersley, late of Fryth in Cowlinge, 1614.

At Wickhambrook a fibula was ploughed up in a field called the Four Acre Honeycomb. Wickhambrook, Hawkedon and Stansfield each holds at least one of those glorious timber-framed houses for which this part of the county is famous. English houses, built of English oaks, in spacious days that were not without fears, set amongst English fields. Is it to be wondered they are so fine a flowering? Happy are we that they have survived, and happy too that later generations have had insight and genius to restore them from neglect the ages had gathered. Hawkedon has Thurston Hall, Stansfield, Swans Hall, and Wickhambrook, Gifford's Hall: with a lesser light in Clopton Hall. If we describe one, we more or less describe the others, of which Gifford's Hall is easily the prime.

There are two Halls of this name, as already mentioned, and may have been owned by the same builder. The one at Stoke by Nayland, built of brick, and this of timber and plaster, moated; an Englishman's home in time of peace.

Its history seems to begin with the Highams of Heighams, whose crest of a rampant horse appears in the ancient glazing of the Hall windows, in alliance with other great names of the Suffolk story. There are remains of an older and probably fortified house not far away. This may have been the residence of Peter Gifford in 1272, who then held the manor rather than the present house. In the fourteenth century the Cloptons were in possession. It naturally passed into several hands, eventually coming to a Thomas Higham through marriage with a female heiress. Whether Thomas rebuilt the existing house in about the middle of the fifteenth century, or his son Clement, died 1521, is not known. One of the Highams, Thomas, reclines in armour in the south of the chancel in the church, described as "The worthy and well deserving Souldier. . . . This Gentleman, in action, before the Cytte of Roan, was shott with a bullett and maymed."

The old malt house has been remodelled to serve as an excellent dining-room, and there is a finely cambered ceiling to the small solar. In another apartment is some excellent Charles II panelling.

The Manor of Thurstanton, Thursturston or Thurston Hall, is mentioned in Domesday. The Hall has been described as "decidedly the best timbered herringbone brickwork house in Suffolk".

Swans Hall, a very considerable gem, with finely carved trails to the bressumers, was held by the Abbot family for many years. It was subsequently purchased by the Stewarts, who held it in 1764. The Reverend Charles Edward Stewart sold it in 1814 to the Reverend Roger Kedington of Rougham, who died in 1818. In 1847 the manor was vested in George Weller Poley, of Boxted Hall.

Woodwork *in excelsis* abounds hereabouts, for at nearby Denston, in an unpretentious little house that once served the chantry priests, is one of the most elaborate and beautiful wooden ceilings extant.

Denston church, although small, has every claim to be described as noble. Once collegiate, it served as a chapel of the College of Priests, founded by John Denston or Derardeston in 1474. It has been suggested that the master mason who conceived the church at Long Melford created also this shrine as a pendant to his genius and a badge of his art. A unique feature is the Robinson tabard, which, with helmet, crest and sword hang in the south chancel aisle.

From here we might pass to Boxted (Anglo-Saxon *box* or *bocsteda*—place of box or beech trees), for long the home of the Poley family, one of the most influential in Suffolk. The Hall, which stands on the west bank of the Gleme, a tributary of the Stour, dates from the latter part of the sixteenth century. It was built by William, son of John Poley, but much external alteration has taken place, destroying the Tudor character. These were probably effected by Mr. George Weller Poley in the eighteenth century.

The most interesting features today are the position, completely moated with a bridge that retains Tudor features, and the spacious hall, wainscoted with sixteenth-century panelling. Beyond the moat runs the Gleme, spanned by a little stone bridge but, as the house is low lying, the water is often a source of trouble in winter.

The Poleys were the progenitors of the Hervey family of Ickworth, through Elizabeth, daughter of John Poley, who in 1554 married William Hervey. They were also linked to nearly all the other landed gentry in the county. Sir John Poley, the last knight of one branch, was chosen burgess of Sudbury without his knowledge, and sat in the Convention against his inclination. There, in a memorable debate, 28th January 1688, as to whether the throne was vacant or no, he made an excellent but characteristic speech.

"Mr. Speaker, I am sent hither to do the church and Caesar right, to vindicate the doctrine of ye one, and preserve the majesty of ye other, both which are in danger from gentlemen's arguments on ye debate this day. Mr. Speaker, here is an affair of the greatest weight before us, both as we are Christians and Englishmen; no less than the deposing a king whom we have sworn allegiance to; will our religions or our laws justifie such a proceeding? I know they will not. Gentlemen, indeed we have laid a mighty stress upon the original contract, and urged the vacancy of the throne from his majesties breach of that, but I hope we shall not proceed rashly on a matter of such consequence to us and our posterity; and therefore I move that this debate be adjourned till ye original contract be produced and laid upon the table for members to peruse, that we may see whether his Majesty has broke it or no."

The church, set on rising ground above the Hall, contains memorials of the family, including recumbent figures in wood to number amongst the rare survivals. These are of William Poley and Alice his wife, inscribed on the cushion beneath the lady's head. There are also memorials to Sir John Poley of Wrongey, and a companion piece to Abigail his wife.

Sitwell says: "In Suffolk too is that monument to a knight of the reign of James I, who is wearing in one ear an earring fashioned in the form of a little golden frog, an emblem that he had been made a Knight of the Danish Order of the Elephant, the oldest Order of Chivalry after the Garter, the import of the jewel being, perhaps, that the elephant and the frog respectively, were the biggest and the smallest quadrupeds known."

Whepstead church is remarkable for its dedication, that of St. Petronella. Formerly the western tower had a leaden spire but it was blown down in an awful storm which raged the night of Oliver Cromwell's death.

When you are at Rede you are on the highest ground in Suffolk, which rises here at 420 feet. The county's best achievement, as M. R. James puts it.

Cockfield, once intimately connected with the Drurys, de Veres and the Springs, is a beautiful, if straggling, piece of Suffolk. It has been called the 'Village of the Greens', and might equally have been dubbed the 'Village of the Halls' and ancient lovely houses that make an English scene. The Romans came here and thought it worth a fight. Their memory and valour is kept green by the name of certain earthworks known as the Warbanks. Nearby have been unearthed coins, tiles and a bronze bust. Breasting the churchyard is an ancient guildhall with brick-nogging and bitten timbers on the north face, and plaster on the south.

The church has been much restored, but one interesting feature is that of the buttresses to the tower that pass through the nave roof. The altar rails, holy table and pulpit, are all of an age-Jacobean. There is also an interesting triple-canopied tomb on the north side of the Sanctuary, known as the Howard tomb. For confirmation of this there is a document that states—'In Cockfield church there in the chauncel a tombe under a wall arched of a Knight Howd, of Sutton's Hall in that towne. He was slaine by his servantes.' The windows contain some old glass, in one panel Anna is shown teaching the BVM to read.

Sad to relate a village legend has it that there are no primroses in Cockfield, neither will they thrive if planted. They were once plentiful, but when the place was depopulated by the plague, they also caught the infection and died, nor have they flourished since that time.

> With its little brimming eye
> And its yellow rims so pale
> And its crisp and curdled leaf—

Who can pass its beauties by
Without a look of love.

Brettenham Hall was for a short time occupied by Joseph Bonaparte, ex-King of Naples and of Spain. He was a brother of Napoleon I. The church of St. Mary has a Stuart choir lectern; and Basket's (Vinegar) Bible dated 1716 is still in use. The river Brett rises in the parish, hence the name.

Felsham church has a very fine fifteenth-century north porch. It is very lofty with exceptional windows for a porch.

There are three Bradfields, of which Bradfield Combust is the most interesting. This was the home of Arthur Young, who died 1820; and a more rural resting place he could not have desired. The church has a twelfth-century font, which was re-cut in the fifteenth century with a cylindrical shaft. But the feature of the church is the two wall paintings in the north-west corner of the nave, one of St. George, the other of St. Christopher. Bradfield St. Clare gets its name from St. Clare Hall, an old moated house that once acted as a retreat for the monks of Bury.

Gedding, hidden away in the hinterland, is noted for its Hall, once completely moated, but now only partially so. The chief feature remaining is the fine old gatehouse, with gabled brick oriels and mullioned windows, much like that at Parham. Built in 1273 by the Geddings, the Hall itself has undergone many alterations, even rebuilding during the fifteenth century, and again as recently as 1897. The gateway has been filled in with windows, thus turning the opening into a spacious room, as at Butley Priory.

The name has been associated not only with the Geddings, but also with the Chamberlaynes, Bokenhams, even the Warennes. A peculiar feature is the flight of steps leading into the moat from the watergate. The reason for this has not been determined.

Like the Hall the ancient church dating from Norman times is also moated. But this may denote the site of a fortification rather than a religious house. Within, are fifteenth-century benches with carved backs and a good font.

Preston lies 2 miles east of Lavenham, holding in the church an ancient font, dating from Norman times and mementoes of its one-time distinguished inhabitant, Robert Reyce, author of the *Breviary of Suffolk*. Gifted in the knowledge of heraldry, he set up in the windows many shields recording Suffolk families, of which large numbers remain. Yet more of his work is to be found in the unusual and beautifully preserved Royal Arms and Table of Commandments. These are triptych in form and when closed appear covered with lengthy pious statements, based on a strong puritan outlook.

The coat of arms of Elizabeth, over the north door, are, in the opinion of Cautley, a rare survival of the arms of Edward VI, adapted for a later reign. The achievement is most remarkable, described at great length by Reyce and of considerable interest to students of heraldry. The Commandments over the south door are of no less interest, because of the idiomatic rendering of 'sarve' for serve and 'murther' for murder.

Preston Hall, or Church Hall Manor, just south of the church, once the home of Reyce, is a fine old half-timbered house, with moulded brick chimneys in clusters that form a characteristic feature.

From here it is but an easy journey westwards to Monks Eleigh, and a cluster of lovely villages, each with its individual beauty. Monks Eleigh, large and beautiful, carries on the tradition by being a woollen town, and bearing about its ways those splendid timber-framed houses, in which the click-clack of the looms must have made music for the passer-by. The fine church of St. Peter in the tree-lined churchyard is set on a hill at the top of a three-square green.

Chelsworth, for utter beauty of thatch and timber-studding, overhangs, and dormers, can hardly be surpassed. On the Brett, bridged by an old brick arch, trees drape a shade, and wood-peckers drum in peaceful harmony. Here is Suffolk in its most typical and satisfying mood. Artists wrought in Chelsworth when wood was the chief medium, and their work remains alive and fair.

The church, a stuccoed building, possesses a clerestoried nave of three bays. The chief interest within is in the wall paintings which have been uncovered, notably the Last Judgement over the

(above) The Chapel of St James at Lindsey

(below) The Church of St Nicholas, Little Saxham

The angel ceiling at Woolpit Church

The panelled roof to the south porch of Kersey Church

A unique chest in Icklingham Church

Hengrave Hall: the royal arms over the main gateway

chancel arch. Opposite this, on the tower arch were two others in the spandrels. That on the south of St. George attacking the Dragon, and that on the north shows the father and mother of the princess watching the proceedings from their palace tower.

The recessed and canopied tomb of Sir John de Philbert, lord of the manor in the fourteenth century, is in a good state of preservation. There is also a fine old iron-bound chest with four hasps and a substantial lock, memorial to blacksmith and carpenter in days of collaboration in craftsmanship and artistry.

Strange to say, in the early years of the nineteenth century, Chelsworth was the scene of barbaric behaviour, when the villagers were obliged to call in the Bow Street Runners for assistance.

Milden's little church has a Norman south door and a slit window in the south wall. It also has a king-post roof to the nave and a few plain benches dated 1685. There is a good monument in the north wall of the chancel to James Allington, 1626.

Bildeston, according to Kirby, is built in a bottom—but it is surely most pleasantly low-lying—out of which has sprung much beauty in a market town, with a huddle of red roofs. It has mellowed with age, prosperity passed, but left lovely in its years. The church, set apart, has several good features, notably a sacriston's room over the south porch, still retaining its curious little wooden gallery for watching the high altar. The tower fell, Ascension Day, 8 May 1975, but little harm was done to the south porch.

Hitcham contains several good houses, including a fine old brick farmhouse on the north side. It also was connected with the woollen trade and has a fine fourteenth-century church with a beautiful hammer-beam roof to the nave. For long Professor Henslow, the botanist and mentor of Darwin, was rector. He was responsible for Darwin going as naturalist on the *Beagle*. The porch was restored to his memory, who did such a great deal to encourage thrift amongst the villagers with his allotment scheme. An old house facing the church has a curious collection of roofs, angles and dormers, with some excellent woodwork within. This, set in a gay old garden, makes an ideal English picture. Semer has a fine three-arched bridge over the Brett. It once had a workhouse, famed far and wide, where the inmates were so well fed as to rival the condition of worthy, but indigent villagers. In fact, it was not so much a workhouse in the accepted meaning of that term, as a factory that worked hard and profitably in the spinning of yarn for Norwich weaving.

Nedging and Naughton, twin children of the Suffolk countryside, are typical peaceful villages that let the world go by. What one lacks the other possesses, thus making a completeness beautiful to contemplate. Nedging church harks back to Norman times, with one of the best north doorways of that period, filled with a pretty eighteenth-century door that looks like a hermit crab set in an alien shell. There are also some ancient but mutilated benches, and a fourteenth-century 'Dawe' bell, inscribed: "John beloved of Christ, be pleased to pray for us." The old Hall, now a farmhouse, is by the green.

> Naughton poor people,
> Sold the bell to build the steeple.

This may explain its one bell in the ancient tower. The church also has a fine old font in which Norman children were baptized, judging by its unusual shape and the intersecting arches that decorate the bowl. There are some old benches, known locally as 'rockers'; can this possibly have reference to powerful preaching?

Naughton Hall is a beautiful old Suffolk home, with dormers in its shingle-tiled roof and fine clustering chimneys.

Whatfield derives, as one might naturally conclude, from Wheatfield. It is a village full of ancient thatched cottages, soft and beautiful amid the changing fields. The old church has a truncated tower, with a cap made of shingle tiles, and a bit of antiquity within in the shape of bench ends, one inscribed: "John Wilson, 1589." There is also a rectory or Hall, moated, that has good woodwork.

Aldham church has a round tower, and not far removed is the memorial to Rowland Taylor:

> Anno 1555
> Dr. Taylor for defending that
> was good, at this place left his blood.

Kersey, referred to in Domesday as "Car's eye", meaning a stream running into a brook, is surely the prettiest and most picturesque village in all Suffolk. It is built on the slopes of a valley of the Brett, the stream crossing the road in the dip, and is crowned on the south side by the beautiful church. One goes out on the northern slope attended by a superb collection of half-timbered, plaster houses of varying gables. Its very name, coupled with Lindsey, is suggestive of comfort, warmth and prosperity, derived from its peculiar genius in the woollen trade. Kersey not only stands for Suffolk at its best and most characteristic self, but for England.

The church, finely sited, also has a porch north and south, with a gloriously decorated panelled roof to the latter, 13 feet by 11 feet, divided into sixteen panels. This was discovered by a former vicar when the plaster false ceiling weakened and had to be attended to. There is a hammer-beam roof to the nave, and a good example of plaster ceiling to the north chapel, decorated with escallop shells (sign of St. James of Compostella), and Tudor roses. This is the Samson chapel, memorial of an ancient family said to have sprung from Abbot Samson of Bury. Its chief treasure is the base of the rood screen, with painted panels in good preservation. There are also remains of wall paintings of St. George; and the stem of the lectern dates from the fifteenth century. It is said that the stone carvings remain unfinished owing to the Black Death which arrested the hands of the mason there engaged.

At the other end of the parish, set on the opposite rise known as Gallows Hill, are the remains of the Priory of St. Mary and St. Anthony. It was founded and endowed by Nesta de Cockfield, who was a guardian of the famous Samson.

The fifteenth-century house by the splash, with a pedimented brick porch of two stages (the window of which was probably brick mullioned), is in pleasing contrast to its plastered front. It adds dignity and grace to the lovely scene. Happy in its position next the tree-draped stream, that is spanned by the little wooden bridge for foot passengers.

If you search carefully, under the eaves of an old house, is a stallion's tail, sign of the age-old calling of horse doctor. A new tail has been recently installed.

And so we pass in an expansive countryside to Lindsey. The church, simple and low and unpretentious, has a little wooden bell-cote and a wooden porch, seared and bitten by the breath of time. Down a step we go as we enter by the south door into an atmosphere of not more recently than the eighteenth century. But that is not all, for close to the highway is an ancient chapel dedicated to St. James, now set in a garden. Yesterday it served as a cow byre, but its origin is lost in time. Probably it was a chantry for Lindsey Castle, and may have been founded by one of the three husbands of Nesta de Cockfield. Certainly it goes back to the Early English period, of which it is a gem, and contains a considerable proportion of early work. Although in all probability it was even then erected on a Norman or earlier foundation. It is still thatched as when a 'Magister' served the simple dimensions of 29 feet by 16 feet, and when a double piscina within a trefoiled arch was not, as now, merely a survival. Note, too, the thatched and ancient White Rose, with the tie-beam jutting out through its pleasant face, and needled by old timber.

And so on to Lavenham, passing *en route* a wonderful little Tudor gateway to Wells Hall Farm at Brent Eleigh. It stands by the quiet roadside in mellowed red brick, with depressed arch and fascinating pinnacles. The timber-framed farmhouse, within an enclosure, is moated, reached by a little bridge. As the Abbey of Bury held much sway hereabouts, this is undoubtedly of ecclesiastical foundation.

As far as Suffolk is concerned all roads lead to Lavenham (Anglo-Saxon Lauvenham-Lafa's Farm). "And in the first place as most nearest unto mee I must goe to the church of Lavenham full of the monuments of the ancient and sometime Lord of that towne the Earle of Oxford, though full many of them within this 40 yeares that I have known them, are worne outt and decayed, which to supply I will now indeavour what I can." So wrote Reyce in his famous *Breviary*.

The centre of the township is the old guildhall of the Corpus Christi Guild, at the corner of Lady Street, and in front stands the market cross. How often in days gone by has this stood sentinel to bull baiting! It consists of a shaft set on steps with, at the top, a cornice of fleurs-de-lis and on the capital a large ball, symbolical of the world. The guildhall, once neglected, has been restored. Inside, rooms ramble into rooms, and underneath are the dungeons. Here, it is said, was housed Hadleigh's martyr, Rowland Taylor.

At the foot of the same street is a fifteenth-century house of rare charm. Here one can rejoice in overhangs supported by those decorated brackets, merging into slender pillars, so characteristic of this Suffolk style of building, with arched, latticed windows and doorways. Opposite is another edition of the guildhall, in the old Wool Hall, an entity in black and white. It has an open roof and timbered gallery, while slots in the great central beam indicate where the wool scales hung. Somewhere in the twenties, this fifteenth-century gem fell into the hands of the house-breakers and all but crossed the Atlantic. Work was actually begun, but spirited local effort prevailed. Scouts were posted along the highways to stop any transport of the fabric, and the building was eventually saved and restored to its present condition.

Then comes the Swan Inn, with its pargetting of fleurs-de-lis. This plaster work is seen on several of these old houses, in which this same motif predominates—with strapwork, squares and circles, conventional flowers and a bishop's mitre, which latter may signify the famous Blaize. These are to be found on the 'Black Lion', the priory and a house in Church Street. Incidentally, the ringers of Lavenham met at the 'Swan' for generations and practised every Tuesday night on sweet-toned handbells that hung up in the bar. The team at one time included three generations of one family.

Is it to be wondered that in such a place Jane Taylor lived, who wrote for children of all time:

> Twinkle, twinkle, little star,
> How I wonder what you are!

While her sister Ann gave us "Meddlesome Matty". You will find their house in Shilling Street, with three gables in the roof—

Shilling Old Grange, where Isaac Taylor, the engraver, and his daughters lived. In 1791 he painted the picture of his two daughters that now hangs in the National Portrait Gallery.

But the glory of Lavenham is the church, and the glory of the church is the tower, which can be seen for miles around. This was built at two periods, between 1486 and 1525, largely from moneys supplied by the de Veres and the Springs. It was later, by a bequest of £200 in 1525, enabled to be carried to its present height, though it was never really completed.

The two families, later united in marriage, conspired together to make this church glorious. The star, or mullet, of the de Veres is seen in the flush flint work, as also the boars on the south porch, supporters of their arms.

Amongst the memorials within is one to William Coppinger. "He was bred a fishmonger in London, so prospering in his profession, that he became Lord Mayor, anno 1512. He gave the half of his estate (which was very great) to pious uses, and relieving the poor." There is also a brass bearing the effigy of a chrysom child and inscription, "Clopton son and heir of Sir Simon D'Ewes, and his wife Anne, a daughter of Sir William Clopton, 1631, aged 10 days".

'In 1868 Mr. James Duncan, a merchant of Mincing Lane, determined to try if he could not establish some method of encouraging the English cultivation of the (beet) root, and of making sugar from it, and with great pluck and spirit erected a sugar factory at Lavenham, in Suffolk, at a considerable expense, hoping thereby to induce the farmers in the neighbourhood to grow the needful supplies. They showed very little hesitation and falling in with his plans, and such success has attended the movement, that the whole district has felt the benefit.' There is an interesting collection of Bygones in the Guildhall, including two sugar-loaf containers, used from 1868 to 1874.

We now move westward to Chedburgh, which has a church that has been rebuilt of white brick, though fourteenth-century windows have been re-used.

Denham near Bury, although only a little church, has one of those remarkable renaissance monuments to Sir Edward Lew-

kenor and Susan his wife, who died of smallpox within two days
of one another in 1605. Another monument with helmet and
crest above, is to Sir Edward's grandson who also died of the
smallpox.

Hargrave is a scattered village with parts over three miles from
the church. The latter which is only 56 feet long is a Norman
building, with the upper part of the rood screen still in position,
placed the wrong way round. It once belonged to Bury Abbey.
The inn is the Cock's Head. Hargrave is of interest in that Southwood Park was bought in 1901, together with the Dalham Hall
estate, by Cecil Rhodes.

Ousden has a Norman church with both north and south doorways of that period, and a central tower which has remained
intact.

Depden church, which has a Norman south doorway and a north
porch, is a seventeenth-century structure made of wood. Within
is a perfect brass to Lady Anne Jermyn, 1572. She was daughter
to Sir Robert Drewry.

Lidgate is famous as having produced John Lydgate the poet
and monk of Bury. His home, an old timber-framed house with
crow-stepped gable, has recently changed hands. Until a few years
ago it was called Suffolk House.

Along the direct road from Bury to Newmarket, at the junction
of the cross roads to Moulton, is one of those interesting graves to
be met with here and there. This is known as the 'Boy's Grave',
and tradition has it that here lies a gipsy or shepherd boy, more
probably the latter, who was tending sheep and wrongfully
accused of having stolen one. This so preyed on his mind that he
hung himself on a nearby tree. The grave is tended by travellers
and local roadmen and is old-world in that bent osiers give it a
cradle-like effect.

At Moulton is a splendid example of a pack-horse bridge that
spans the Kennett and probably connected Bury with Cambridge
in the old days.

Recently, at Gazeley, a tower mill, built of brick about 100
years ago, was sold as a desirable residence. It stood derelict for
some years until bought in 1947 and remodelled under the super-

vision of an architect. The walls are 3 feet thick at the base. The upper rooms give a wonderful view over the surrounding countryside. Higham was carved out of the civil parish of Gazeley in 1861, and consists of Upper, Lower and Middle Green. Newmarket is part in Suffolk and part in Cambridgeshire, but wholly in the former for administration purposes. Its suitability for racing is thought to have been discovered by the exercising of Spanish horses, survivors of the Armada. They were brought over from Galloway, where they were cast ashore and brought here to gallop on the heath. The town consists of one long street, the north side of which is in Suffolk and the other in Cambridgeshire.

About 1½ miles westward is a curious earth-work, known as the Devil's Dyke, of which Kirby remarks—"by the vulgar so called who readily ascribe to him what they cannot account for". It has been attributed to Uffa, and is thought to have been a boundary between the East Angles and the Mercians. Now it serves to divide the dioceses of Norwich and Ely.

Dalham Hall, standing on the highest ground in the county, is not without interest. Built of red brick at the end of the seventeenth century, or the beginning of the eighteenth century by Simon Patrick, Bishop of Ely, it partakes of the happy character of that period. A tradition runs that the bishop intended another floor, as he liked to be able to see his cathedral; but that was never accomplished. What he probably intended was a gazebo or cupola, which would have added considerably to the appearance of the place. Standing four-square, attended by its harmoniously designed stabling in the midst of parklands, within shadow of its church and adorned with terrace walks, it has an air of spaciousness that may have recommended it to one so accustomed to African vistas as Cecil Rhodes. He intended to make it his English home.

Barrow was the home of the Heighams, and a canopied tomb of Sir Clement Heigham is on the north wall of the chancel of the church, which has a Norman window.

Bereft of worldly lyfe in hope to ryse to endless light,
By Christ's deserts, here rest the corse of Clement Heigham, Knight.

A number of brasses, with effigies and coats of arms are on the back of the tomb. When Queen Elizabeth made her progress through the county, she stayed at Barrow Hall. This was a large brick building surrounded by a moat. It was demolished towards the end of the eighteenth century.

Little Saxham delights in one of the most interesting churches in this area, particularly as regards its tower, said to be the best of all round towers. It certainly rivals that of Thorington on the other side of the county, with its finely preserved Norman arcading at the top stage. This consists of four semi-circular arched windows of two lights recessed; and between these are pairs of arched recesses all rising from a string course. Narrow slit-like openings are on the outward face and there is a battlemented top. The tower batters up to the sill of the upper stages and then rises perpendicularly. The most notable feature within is the tower arch, a beautiful Norman opening that rises some 17 feet high and is only 4 feet 6 inches wide. South of this is a Norman arched recess, which may have been an opening. The south doorway is also Norman, with a billet mould, suggestive of a very early and beautiful structure. The benches are mostly fifteenth century, and there is a most interesting specimen of a bier, with folding handles and decorated legs that dates from Jacobean days.

Saxham Hall was for long the home of the Lucases and Crofts. It stood on the Bury road, a quarter of a mile from the church. Charles II visited it more than once. A seat in the church with an acorn carved in a poppy head is said to commemorate his visits.

In Great Saxham there is a Palladian mansion, built 1798, which was preceded by Nutmeg Hall. So called from John Eldred its builder, who introduced into this country that condiment so highly esteemed in his day as a carminative. He figures in Hakluyt's "The Voyage of Mr. Eldred to Trypolis, in Syria by sea, and from thence by land and river to Babylon and Balsara, 1583".

Ickworth Hall, situated in a park of 1,800 acres, surrounded by many fine trees, with a circuit of 11 miles round its borders, might be considered a magnificent folly. Built about 1796 by Frederick Hervey (1730–1803), fourth Earl of Bristol and Bishop of Derry, it has been described as the most remarkable and eccentric of the great Suffolk houses.

Frederick Hervey was, perhaps, the most outstanding member of the family. It might be recalled that Lady Mary Wortley Montague said that society consisted of three classes of human beings, 'men, women and Herveys'. He was first a lawyer, then a priest, bishop, earl and popular figure, philanthropist, art lover, traveller, geologist, agriculturist and friend of Arthur Young. He was also a gallant whose escapades were but thinly veiled. Added to these he had a passion for building houses on a magnificent scale.

In due time (1779) he succeeded to the Hervey estates, and set a plan in motion for a new home. The family, who had lived at Ickworth since 1467, had for generations occupied the Lodge, a large farmhouse type of building; but this was too small and mean for the new Earl. In July 1788 he records in his diary that "Sir John Vanbrugh came to Ickworth and sett out ye scituation of my new house, leaving a plan with me for ye same". The building was eventually placed in the charge of two brothers, Francis Sandys, the architect, and the Rev. Joseph Sandys as Clerk of the Works.

Soon after, Hervey left England for Italy, and never again set foot in this country. He therefore never saw a stone laid of his great conception, and died in almost distressed circumstances in 1803 of gout in the stomach. Some months later his body was brought home to Ickworth for interment.

The rotunda, the central feature of this fine sweep of buildings, extending to 600 feet in length, is over 100 feet high. It is composed of two orders, Ionic and Corinthian, and has an Ionic portico on the north-east side. This is surmounted by a balustrade, designed to hide the chimneys. The corridors are quadrants of circles, curving out northwards from the centre, with an intended wing at each end, of which only one has been executed, the present western mansion.

The gardens, surrounded by the Great Terrace, are very beautiful. The terrace itself, commanding a fine sweep of the park, has outwardly a low brick wall with a stone coping, and inwardly a rounded box hedge, while the gardens are laid out with balustrades, steps, urns and vases. They contain also many fine cypresses, yews and perennial shrubs, with deep yew and box hedges, set amid the level lawns.

The church contains much of interest, notably some panels of foreign glass in the windows. Here, too, is the only example in the county of the royal arms done in embroidery, 52 inches wide, and dating from the time of George I.

Chevington, not far removed, has a good deal of interest. The church shows late Norman work in north and south doorways and has an early wooden south porch. The nave roof is of the king-post variety. There are some good poppy heads, with figures of musicians. And, not least, a noble Gothic chest of the fourteenth century that resembles one at Hacconby, Lincolnshire. It has wide stiles that are extended to form feet, decorated with subjects out of the bestiaries. Unfortunately the right-hand stile has been removed to meet a bell ringer's-convenience. If one compares this with the specimen at Icklingham All Saints, which is contemporary, a most interesting variation of treatment is apparent. This splendid locker was shown at the Exhibition of Medieval Art held at South Kensington in 1930.

At the upper end of the north side of the nave a stone coffin was found containing the perfect skeleton of a young ecclesiastic. The hands were raised on the breast and the remains of a leaden chalice, which had fallen from them, lay near the right shoulder.

Chevington, part of the estate of Britwulf, was conferred upon the Monastery of Bury by William the Conqueror. Owing to its position it soon became a favourite retreat of the abbots. On the Dissolution it passed to the Kytsons, who treated it in like manner, erecting a hunting lodge in the park. The site of the Hall is now a farmhouse, the deep moat and high ramparts remaining.

Hawstead, 4 miles south-west of Bury, was the home of the Drury's, who gave their name to Drury Lane, their London house. The family was very distinguished, one member formed part of the retinue of Henry VIII at the Field of the Cloth of Gold and attended Cardinal Wolsey when he received Charles V at Dover in 1522. Another was at the siege of Rouen when only 16 years of age and received his spurs on the field from the Earl of Essex. The Sir Robert who married Anne, daughter of Sir Nicholas Bacon of Red-

grave, became the patron of Dr. Donne. It is his daughter, Elizabeth, who reclines above her tomb against the south wall of the
chancel in the church. She is said to have died from a box on the
ears. Her epitaph, "finely written in gold upon jett", is by Donne:

> Her pure and eloquent blood,
> Spoke in her cheeks, and so distinctly wrought
> That one might almost say her body thought.

She is said to have gained the affection of Prince Henry, son of
James I.

The issue failing, the estates passed to the Cullums, in whose
family it remained until within recent years. The Reverend Sir
John Cullum became the historian of the parish and its antiquarian in a volume of great merit, published in 1784. Many of
the family's beautiful mementoes are now to be seen in Moyses
Hall. Hawstead Place was pulled down in 1830. Place farm stands
on its site. The old Rectory House was pulled down about the
middle of the nineteenth century.

Hawstead church, with its two Norman doorways, is distinguished for its memorials, the earliest of which is a cross-legged
knight, who lies under a canopy in the north wall. He is believed
to be Sir Eustace Fitz Eustace, Lord of the Manor in the time of
Henry III. There is a Nicholas Stone bust of Sir William Drury, in
armour, father of the last male representative, for which the
sculptor received £140.

Hardwick House was purchased by Sir Robert Drury, the last of
that line, after the death of his daughter, because he could no
longer reconcile himself to his ancestral home. This in time passed
to the Cullums and was partially rebuilt in 1681. At one time a
special breed of sheep fed from its pastures said to have descended
from the noted flock kept by the Abbey of Bury.

Horringer, formerly called Horringsheath, is the subject of a
book by Manners W. Hervey, from which I cannot refrain from
quoting.

> Coming up the street, over the village green, I see them all, the
> keepers and the labourers; the latter clad in smocks, the former
> in velvet frocks. The men wear tall hats, very rough, some white,

some black. The boys too are dressed in smocks. The velvet frocks are black and brown. The men wear buskins. The smocks are prettily embroidered in blue or red on the breast, and on the short sleeves. None of them wear collars, or cloth, but neckerchiefs. They are proud of their gay smocks and tall hats.

Inside the church . . . the venerable form of the Rev. Henry Hasted, rector here from 1814 to 1852, is to be seen in the pulpit. In the gangway during service time a man stands with a long wand of office. He is one of two beadles. . . . The other was in the gallery where the choir sang. At service time these two changed places. Their business was to restrain the young, and to keep the somnolent awake. They were called Stick men. They wore duffel coats with capes and their coats are bound with yellow braid.

Nowton church has a large quantity of Flemish glass consisting almost entirely of medallions in yellow satin or enamel. None is older than the beginning of the sixteenth century, but some are of excellent quality. One rare subject is a scene from the passion of St. Christopher, a red-hot helmet being put on his head.

Great and Little Whelnetham might be taken together. The church of St. Thomas à Becket at the former has a wooden belfry, erected in 1749, "at the cost of James Merest". The Crouched, Crutched or Crossed Friars had one little house here.

Rushbrooke Hall must be written of as in the past tense. It was similar in character to Melford and Kentwell, and was the moated home of the Jermyns. The little church, set just within the park gates, is of great interest, furnished with gabled stalls facing each other like a college chapel. It suggests the 'godly chapel of synging men', although one must not be led away by the elaborate organ front that crowns the west end, for it is but a sham. Neither does the furnishing date from those early days, for the legend has it that a former owner of the Hall dismantled his drawing-room for the purpose, using all the panelling. The most conspicuous feature is the Arms of Henry VIII, placed in position at the junction of nave and chancel. Munro Cautley says: "These must be those erected in our churches after the Reformation, and so far as I am aware, the only example of this period in the county."

On Rougham Common were discovered some antiquities from tumuli. Two burials of the Roman period were found in brick chambers. One of these remains *in situ*, and a model is in the British Museum. The church is handsome, with a battlemented western tower, and a battlemented nave and aisles. There is also a hammer-beam roof, and some old glass.

A Rougham father, Mr. G. Lebbon, and his son Ian collect old farming wagons, coaches and pony traps. When the necessary repairs are done in bringing them back to life again they are exhibited at county shows throughout the country. What a wonderful hobby and work of preservation of these old landships.

And so we pass to Hessett, a pleasant village of characteristic Suffolk cottages surrounding its lovely church, itself set amid a beautiful God's acre. Beneath trees, the stones lean and slant over the ancient dead, for here are some of the oldest grave memorials and the remains of a churchyard cross. Within the church are a number of extremely interesting wall paintings, amongst which is a Tree of the Seven Deadly Sins. In this instance the lower part represents Christ surrounded by all kinds of tools—sword, shears, hammer, scythe-blade, cart-wheel, spoon, gridiron, harrow, shovel, pitchfork, jug (or dice-box) and a playing card (the six of diamonds). This is one of those portrayals described as the Christ of the Trades, thought to represent the sanctifying of labour. Or, perhaps judging from the playing card, it is a pictorial rendering of the implements connected with the Passion.

There is some good old glass here, in one window a boy with a golf club. Then there are two Maries, with their children, relics of the Last Judgement, and the story of Katherine. But the chief treasures are rarities indeed: a painted linen burse to hold the Host, one side bearing the face of Christ and the Evangelistic emblems and, on the other, the Pascal Lamb. There is also a lace-work cloth, thought to be a cover for a Pyx canopy, 2 feet 4 inches square, fringed with silk. In the centre is a hole one inch in diameter. The fifteenth-century screen has been repainted and there are a lot of early benches.

The village inn has a brick pier to carry its sign of 'Five Bells', which is unusual and noteworthy. Drinkstone, the next parish, has a beautiful fifteenth-century screen, shorn of its vaulting, with tracery and remains of colour, and a notable font. The old red-brick tower stands serene amid the trees. A few years ago there were two windmills, smock and post.

This brings us to Woolpit, and the realm of folk-lore and fairy. Its very name is suggestive, derived from the wolves pit that is said to have existed in these fields. It is, like all its neighbours, old-world and full of charm, with delightful timber-framed houses that sag and spread beside its ways. Woolpit was the scene of one of the old Horse Fairs that began on 6th September and lasted a week.

In King Stephen's days, out from the wolf-pit came two children, waifs from St. Martin's land, where it is always twilight. They were found by harvesters (so it was high summer) and taken to the house of Sir Richard de Culne, when it was observed they were quite human, though their skin was of a greenish hue. Not at once could they unfold their tale but, being kindly treated and provided with the only food they could eat, namely beans, they told how (like children) they had wandered into a cavern where they heard the sound of bells that lured them on. In the excitement of trying to trace the music they found themselves in Woolpit, the land of bright light across the broad river. And the cavern had closed behind them. They continued to live with Sir Richard, but soon the boy died; when she was of age the girl married a man from King's Lynn. Where, we may ask, are her descendants today? The story is vouched for by Ralph of Coggeshall (land of the green fingers) and William of Newburgh.

Is it to be wondered therefore that in Woolpit is a well, situated in a meadow near the church—'Our Lady's Well', to which pilgrims came for an eye salve; neither has it lost its efficacy. It is averred that over the sacred spot was a chapel but, like the green children, this has entirely vanished. This was all part and parcel of 'Our Lady of Woolpit', an image in the church of miraculous powers, situated in the Lady Chapel, under a rich canopy.

But if it is famed for all these things, so it was famed for a white brick produced in its kells. These, as M. R. James reminds us, have defaced many a country mansion, and some were even sent to Russia for "the Emperor to look at".

The glory of Woolpit, however, is its church, a unique and

almost perfect survival of pre-Reformation splendour. The assembly and magnificence of the woodwork is revealed in the double hammer-beam roof to the nave, the splendid aisle roofs, and the truly wonderful benches, almost perfectly preserved. The latter consist of two sets of thirteen benches, giving fifty-two bench-ends in all, embellished with animals on the extensions, of which none is missing. The carved backs of the westernmost benches are a glory of workmanship, decorated with quatrefoils within circles. The backs of the benches in general are clearly carved in a similar fashion. The nave roof bears angels, eleven a side, while the helves are wrought into niches filled with figures of saints, supported by angels with outstretched wings. There is a good fifteenth-century screen with newly painted panels of saints, worthily done, and above is a novel and beautiful canopy of honour for the rood, executed in wood. The choir stalls are also good, and amongst the embellishments is a figure of the Virgin with her pot of lilies. There is also a brass or lateen lectern said to have been the gift of the Virgin Queen. It has a slot in the beak to receive coins, and an opening in the tail to extract them.

There was a chapel of St. James in the north aisle, mentioned in a will of one John Bawde, 1501: "That he desires the trene [woodwork] of the altar be well and sufficiently painted (which I did make) and cloth to be bought to cover the same." The stool (bench), which he had also made, was to be coloured and garnished with scallops and other signs of St. James. So then this glorious woodwork of Woolpit may be of local genius.

It is rumoured that one of the monks who served Woolpit travelled from Bury on a donkey and tethered his animal in a field still known as Monk's Close. But this must be considered one of the far-fetched tales, as it is a good ass's journey from Bury.

Elmswell has a splendid tower, with probably the finest flint devices of wheels, lily pots and sacred monograms in the county. There is also a very fine memorial to Sir Robert Gardiner, 1619, done by Colt. His badge was a tiny rhinoceros, which vies with the frog ear-rings at Boxted.

And thus to Rattlesden mentioned by Lydgate·

A newe cherche he dyde edefye
Ston brought from Kane [Caen] out of Normandye
By the Se, and set upon the strande
At Ratylsdene, and carried forth bi lande.

This suggests that Rattlesden was once a port and the stone that came from Caen to build the Abbey Church of Bury was landed here. The stream now would hardly bear such a burden.

The church, of ancient foundation, is all but new within, but it has a magnificent hammer-beam roof, with elaborate cresting and finely-moulded cornice. There are eleven sets of six angels (new) to grace and beautify the whole. The screen is a perfect reproduction of an East Anglian type, complete with rood loft and rood with attendant figures. There is also a triple-faced poppy head of considerable interest.

Beyton, not far removed, possesses one of the four round towers to be found in the western half of the county. It is of considerable interest in that it has buttresses, the only instance. These old towers stand unaided by props and this exception proves the rule.

Tostock has some good benches including a unicorn and a pelican, and a fourteenth-century font with floriated panels. In the churchyard was a gravestone to Thomas Chapman, who died at the age of 111, and Elizabeth his wife, who died aged 95 in 1753.

Pakenham has a fine transeptal church that stands high, evidence of an early foundation or fortified site. It has Norman doorways. Ancient indeed is the lovely old village that clusters around its elevated shrine. Many signs of man's early habitation and industry have been found here. Under the shadow of the spreading mulberry tree on the vicarage lawn, in a dummy upper window of the old house, is something of modern interest. It is a piece of Rex Whistler's work, executed in an hour or so in careless abandon. He was stationed here with the Scots Guards. One wet day he painted the figure of an eighteenth-century parson, bewigged, sitting reading by candle-light. As he worked a brother officer held an umbrella to screen him from the weather. Here is the finest mill in the county, its white sails still gleaming in the sun. Turning slightly northwards we come to Stowlangtoft. The

name really derives from the great Norman family of Langetot-
their Stow. The fine and lofty church, unusual in its dedication to
St. George, stands within a double entrenchment and contains
many fine features, particularly the Flemish carving in the chancel,
which includes the Harrowing of Hell. The great jaw with its den-
tured curve opens to let the sinners pass in, while above looms
the eye. The choir stalls are really beautiful, old mellowed oak
worked in Gothic arches and roundels, buttressed and traceried.
The misericords are also good. The bench-ends are complete, each
arm with a beast on it. There is an iron-studded door within the
magnificent south porch and the font is adorned with saints. This
was the home of the Maitland Wilsons.

Great Barton had a fine old square Hall, originally built by
Robert Audley early in the seventeenth century, but greatly
enlarged by the Bunburys. Henry W. Bunbury, the caricaturist,
was a member of the family. Sir Charles Bunbury was the owner
of the first winner of the Derby, with Diomed in 1780, and the
horse was buried in the park. Great Barton won the Walter Horne
Trophy for the best-kept village in 1970, largely because of miles
and miles of beautifully-kept hedges.

The risings and fallings of the water of Barton Mere were sup-
posed to govern the price of corn, according to a Suffolk legend.
In the drought of 1868, when it dried up, the Reverend Harry
Jones thought he had discovered a lake dwelling.

Ixworth is a place of some antiquity, for quite a number of
relics have been unearthed within its borders. The fine old wooden-
walled Water Mill is a happy survival, but in need of restoration.
There is an old house in the one street that still bears ridge-tiles
and another with pargetting on its sagging front.

The church of St. Mary is old and good, with flint work without,
and a tower inscription that can be deciphered: "Master Robert
Schot, Abbot". He was Abbot of Bury in 1470–3. There is a renaissance tomb to Robert Codrington (1567), north of the altar. On
the north side of the churchyard is a stone commemorating Phillip
Pilbrow, who died 18th June 1750, aged 101.

> There are but few who do my years exceed,
> I to the last, the smallest print could read.

I ne'er was Blooded, nor did Physic try,
God gave me health to live, to him I die.

At Barningham the innkeeper of the 'Royal George' sported one of those rhyming signs that were sometimes met with. Note the Suffolk idiom.

William Allen live here,
Sells spiritous liquors & good home brewed beer.

Stanton has two churches. All Saints contains a beautiful ogee tomb-arch and a south tower which is now in ruins. St. John's, now disused, must have been a fine building, with still remaining fine and lofty fourteenth-century windows. But the two parishes had four inns: 'The George', Cock Inn, 'Rose and Crown', and the 'Three Horseshoes'.

On the south wall of the nave of Walsham-le-Willows church hangs an 'In Memoriam' garland or crant, to the memory of Mary Boyce, who died a virgin at 20 in 1685. It was customary for boys and girls to hang a garland here on the anniversary of her death. Cricket bats are made at this village.

Hepworth has a church that was burnt out a few years ago, but they managed to save the font cover, a remarkable and beautiful piece of work which has been badly patched up. In the lower stages are canopies with men looking out of castle doors. In the will of William Mordeboice, blacksmith of Hepworth, written in his own hand: "28th. January, Anno Regni Caroli nostri the Xixth. annoq. dni 1644. Item i doe give and bequeath unto Rose my daughter . . . such . . . linen as is belonging to infants at their time of baptism."

Badwell Ash has but one son to its credit—Attorney General, Lord Thurloe. The church of St. Mary is a fine structure with clerestoried nave, south aisle, chancel and fine south porch; but within it has no feature of interest save the excellent font. One peculiar external item is to be found on the south-east buttress, in a set of blacksmith's tools, with two horse-shoes, and letters which might be 'R.B.'.

Badwell Ash Hall is a fine old Tudor brick building with mullioned windows, transomed, crow-stepped gables, pinnacles and moulded brick chimneys. Within is a fine carved staircase of oak that mounts up to the roof. Here, too, is a Moat Farm standing in sedgy waters, peaceful reminder of all the summers that have passed over its faded walls.

Norton is a name to conjure with, at least so thought Henry VIII, when, in an impecunious state, he came here to strike his claim at gold mining, though his efforts were fruitless. The workings were visible to within recent years, pointed out by the old inhabitants.

Camden in his *Britannica* speaks thus: "I know not whether I should have taken notice into what vain and groundless hopes of finding gold at Norton, king Henry the Eighth was drawn by a credulous kind of avarice; but the diggings there speak for me."

And here is an extract from a 'Household Book' referring to the venture—"july 1538, Item, paid to William Wade, servant to Sir Piers Edgecombe, Knight, LXs, for his cost and expense bringing up hither from Cornwall, at his own charge, Manuel George and William Wynget, miners, to be sent at this time into Suffolk, to try and work the new mine."

Little Haugh Hall, a mellow old house in this parish, was the home of the Milesons, from whom it passed to the Edgars, who in turn sold it to Thomas Macro, the wealthy grocer of Bury St. Edmunds. The third son of this line was the celebrated Dr. Cox Macro (1683–1757), Fellow of Christ's College, Cambridge. He is reputed to have asked a friend for a suitable motto for his arms, who suggested without hesitation—"Cocks may Crow".

The church of Norton is fine within, if somewhat plain without, and possesses one of the best of the Suffolk fonts, which has survived almost intact. Here, too, are benches and bench-ends in good order. But perhaps the misericordes of the choir stalls are the more notable, with a fine example of the martyrdom of St. Edmund. The artist craftsman has made quite sure of the saint's demise. There is another of St. Andrew and one of a Pelican in her Piety. Some of the old glass remains in the tracery lights. The chancel is the oldest part of the fabric and has a collar-braced roof, with wide cornices that appear to have been coloured. There is good iron work on the vestry door, and an old chest marked, "T.B.S.B. 1604".

Great Ashfield church has an exceptionally fine Stuart pulpit, square, standing on huge bulbous legs and complete with back and sounding board. It is inscribed "W.F." and dated 1619. Of the same period is the Holy Table, the panelling behind it and the chest in the vestry.

Wattisfield has been noted for pottery, much esteemed in the old days for dairy and gardeners' purposes. The church of St. Margaret has both north and south porches, the former a simple sixteenth-century wooden structure and the latter of stone. One of the bells has a quaint couplet.

W.L.T.D. IN THE RAYNE
OF QUENE ELSBETH BIS XIII.

The initials are those of the founders, Land and Draper, and twice thirteen refers to the date of the casting 1584, being the twenty-sixth year of Elizabeth's reign.

Rickinghall Inferior has a very fine church with a round tower, dating from the twelfth century, and a delightful fifteenth-century octagon top. There are two windows with beautiful tracery, one south and one at the east end.

Hinderclay church has a Ringers' Gotch that holds about two gallons. It is inscribed:

By Sam Moss this Pitcher was given to the Noble Society of Ringers at Henderclay in Suffolk. Thomas Sturgeon, Edwd Lock, John Hans, Rich Ruddock & Rd. Chapman. To which Society he once belonged 7 years and left in y one thousand seven hundred & 2.

From London I was sent
As plainly doth appear
It was with this intent
To be fild with strong beer.

Pray remember the Pitcher when empty.

It is said of Coney Weston church that it is a complete and interesting example of fourteenth-century work. There is no tower, as this fell many years ago. Knettishall's little church has become a ruin, and much of the furnishings have been removed to Riddlesworth, across the border.

Hopton is on the Little Ouse and the borders of Norfolk. The church of All Saints has a good deal of interest. The door to the tower stairs in the south aisle is ironclad, and so is a huge fourteenth-century chest, 87 inches long. The clerestory is of Tudor brick and the late medieval nave roof is of great interest. It is a hammer-beam with recumbent figures wearing ermine collars, holding musical instruments, chalice and books. The whole roof is coloured.

Barningham church has some splendid benches, equal to any we have met with before, and also a screen. There is a slip of wood on which is painted in fifteenth-century letters a reference to the Scourging, the Trinity and the Entombment. M. R. James says it was part of an altar-piece composed of three Nottingham alabaster tablets.

Bardwell has another of the splendid churches about this part, which can be seen a long way off. It is a memorial to Sir William Bardwell who died 1434. His portrait in glass can be seen in one of the north side windows. Wall paintings were discovered at a restoration in 1853, and as quickly covered over again with whitewash. But not before they were copied in colour. They can be seen in Volume 2 of the *Proceedings* of the Suffolk Institute of Archaeology.

The old Hall stands by the road south of the village and has a beautiful brick front.

Ixworth Thorpe is a small village on the Thet. The little thatched church has something of a tower which ends in a wooden belfry. But inside are some of the most interesting of the bench-ends. These include a thatcher with his comb, a lady leading a little dog, a unicorn and a mermaid. The Tudor brick south porch is interesting.

9

Villages of the Suffolk Brecklands

On busy streets and sylvan-walks between,
Fen, marshes, bog and heath all intervene;
Here pits of crag, with spongy, plashy base,
To some enrich th' uncultivated space:
For there are blossoms rare, and curious rush,
The gale's (candleberry) rich balm, and sun-dew's crimson blush
Whose velvet leaf with radiant beauty dress'd,
Forms a gay pillow for the plover's breast.

BRECKLAND is a unique stretch of country in East Anglia,
with a local name derived from Breck, sandy open fields. It com-
prises nearly 400 square miles of which 253 are in Norfolk and 145
in Suffolk, and once was one of the most thickly populated districts
in England. Now it is the most sparsely peopled of any area, 82 to
the square mile in 1926. Anciently known as the Fielding it was
named Breckland in 1895 by the late W. G. Clarke who was the
great authority on the district, which he knew and loved so well.
This baptism is comparable to Poppyland, the district about
Cromer, a name given by Clement Scott.

H. J. Massingham in a percipient appreciation of Clarke's
book—*In Breckland Wilds*, says this of him:

> This strange land Clarke knew off by heart and by head. There
> was nothing he didn't know about it. Every insect, every bird, every
> mollusc, every flower, nearly every rabbit—he knew where they
> were, why they were there, how they lived, how many of them
> were there and how many would be there in the future. Fauna,
> flora, geology, rainfall, physical geography, archaeology, village
> history, their knowledge streamed out of him, and every mortal

thing that crept, grew, ran, lay or stood on the beloved heaths he
walked with so springy a step he knew as well as though their
area had been 400 inches instead of miles.

Breckland consisted of a loose soil in a comparatively treeless
country until the middle of the eighteenth century, and was the
nearest approach in England to steppe conditions. In 1610 the
Duke of Wurtemberg came to Thetford with the King; they
coursed the hare, flew a hawk and caught dotterels. It was noted
for one species of bird, the ringed plover. There was a great sand-
storm at Downham in 1668, when the sand travelled five miles
from Lakenheath Warren, almost overwhelming the village, and
for a long time blocking the course of the Little Ouse. Downham
subsequently obtained the prefix of Sandy, now changed to Santon. Which reminds one of the tale about the farmer when asked
in what parish was his farm? He scratched his head and remarked,
"Sometimes in Norfolk and sometimes in Suffolk. It depends
which way the wind blows." Since 1840, however, trees have been
planted in enormous numbers, Scotch pine, larch, spruce, silver
birch, elm and oak. But of recent years much has been done by
the Forestry Commission, lining up the regimented and alien
conifers.

Clarke recorded that many of the crops provided a prodigality
of colour—the bright yellow of the mustard, the orange of the
kidney vetch, the cream of the buckwheat, the purple of the tares
and lucerne, the gold of melilot and black medick, the pink of
sainfoin, the delicate rose-pink and the brilliant carmine of
tobacco, red of Italian clover and the white of the Dutch.

The villages and fields are larger than those elsewhere. In the
old days men could plough straight for twenty furlongs. Mildenhall
is the largest flat area in Suffolk and Lakenheath comes next.

A number of plants flourish here and hardly anywhere else, the
special 'Breck' species numbering nineteen. These range from the
Conical and Spanish catch-fly to Boehmer's phleum; and there are
many rare flowers, including the prickly lettuce and the pasque
flower.

Bird life is very full, for within six miles of Thetford 196 species
have been recorded and many have local names. For example the

district known as Poppylot derives from popeler, an old term for a spoonbill. Clarke writes of a night spent at Santon Downham— "I remember one night there at the end of May when all the stone curlews of the neighbourhood shrieked from dusk to dawn, night-jars churred from every belt, ringed plovers whistled as they changed quarters and the plaint of many lapwings was rarely stilled. Before dawn the cuckoos and the snipe had started and with the first gleam of daylight 'all the little birds that are' filled the air 'with their sweet jargoning'."

There are, or were, some twenty-nine barrows in Suffolk Breckland, viz., Blood Hill and Santon; Hill of Health at Culford; How Hill at Eriswell; Deadman's Grove at Icklingham; Seven Hills at Ingham; Hut Hill at Lackford; Maid's Cross Hill at Lakenheath; Jennet's Hill at West Stow and Traveller's Hill at Wordwell.

We might now proceed to look in at the villages, taking all those north of the Bury-Newmarket road and as far east as Euston. First then comes Kentford on the Kennett, which has an inn with the peculiar name of the Fox and Ball. The church including the tower is almost entirely fourteenth century, and has a small rose window in the west wall of the tower, which is unusual.

Risby has a round tower of Norman date, with slit windows north and south. There is also some old glass, a screen of great merit and wall paintings. There are several barrows in this parish.

There are three Fornhams. All Saints has an inn called the Three Kings. Not far removed is the hill which gives its name to the hundred of Thingoe-the Thing-how, or hill of assembly. Here also is the site of the Franciscan priory of Babwell, where the Friars settled after having been ejected from Bury. A nice old house marks the spot, but is not as old as the priory. In the church is a brass to the memory of Thos. Barwick, a professor of medicine at Bury St. Edmunds.

Fornham St. Martin church has an ancient misericord of the martyrdom of St. Thomas of Canterbury, worked into a modern lectern, and another of the legend of St. Martin (the dedicatory saint), worked into a reading desk. The inn is The Wool Pack.

Fornham St. Genevieve is the scene of the defeat of the Flemish army which, under the command of the Earl of Leicester, landed on the Suffolk coast near Walton (Felixstowe), and proceeded to war against Henry II. They were routed here on the banks of the Lark, by Chief Justice Lucy and Humphrey de Bohun. According to Bloomfield the historian, the slain lie under the Seven Hills, their captain amid them. Carlyle wrote:

> For the river Lark, though not very discernable, still runs or stagnates in that county; and the battle ground is there; serving at present as a pleasure-ground to his Grace of Northumberland. Copper pennies of Henry II are still found there—rotted out from the pouches of poor slain soldiers, who had not time to buy liquor with them. In the river Lark itself was fished up, within man's memory, an antique gold ring, which fond Dilletantism can almost believe may have been the very ring Countess Leicester threw away, in her flight, into that same Lark river or tree ditch. Nay, a few years ago, in tearing out an enormous super annuated ash tree, now grown quite corpulent, bursten, superfluous, but long a fixture in the soil, and not to be dislodged without a revolution—there was laid bare, under the roots, 'a circular mound of skeletons, wonderfully complete' all radiating from a centre, faces upwards, feet inwards; evidently the fruits of battle; for many of the heads were cleft or had arrow holes in them.

The church was burnt down on 24th June 1782, "through the recklessness of a man shooting at jackdaws".

Hengrave Hall, one of the most satisfying and beautiful remnants of Tudor architecture left in this county, was built by Sir Thomas Kyston, kt., between the years 1525 and 1538. The latter date on the building testifies to an accomplishment of which the originator might well feel proud, after having obtained a licence to build and embattle his house. Unlike many of its contemporaries in Suffolk, it is built largely of stone, in a land where no stone is available. This was brought at great expense and labour by land and water from the quarries at King's Cliff in Northamptonshire, via Worlington and Brandon. The remainder was supplied by the dissolved abbeys of Ixworth, Burwell, and Thetford. Part, however, is of brick, from the brick-fields of Bury Abbey, baked to a yellowy whitish colour, to tone with the freestone. Timber was supplied from the nearby parks of Comby, and Sowe or Southwood. Lead came from Ixworth priory, and some from the offices of the dissolved abbey of Bury.

Sir Thomas Kytson, or 'Kytson the Merchant', was a member of the Merchant Adventurers' Company of London, and immensely rich. His business was extensive in merchandise from the great cloth fairs and staples of Flanders, and he held property and estates elsewhere in Suffolk; also in Devon, Dorset, Somerset and Nottingham. The house he built was larger by a third than the Hall as we see it today, and moated. In the seventeenth century considerable alterations were made and the outer court was removed. Then in 1775, a mass of buildings which projected on the east and north sides, together with a high tower, were demolished and the moat was filled up.

It is, then, the stately quadrangle that remains, a fine example of domestic architecture. It resembles Oxborough and Blickling in Norfolk, in the treatment of turrets; that of Henry VII's Chapel at Windsor; King's College, Cambridge; the Choir at Winchester; the Gatehouse of Brasenose College, Oxford; and St. George's, Windsor.

The most interesting feature is the beautiful gateway, unique in its conception, illustrating the introduction into this country of the Renaissance, and blending it with earlier Tudor without a discordant note. The deep archway has finely moulded jambs, and spandrels filled with the unicorn crest of the Kytsons; while the oriel, beautiful and perfect with its segmental windows, rises on a multitude of mouldings, enriched and supported at its base by the Royal Arms. The domes are richly adorned with crockets and scale work, which the slender shafts between the lights terminate below in sculptured bosses.

The chapel, to the left of the gateway, which is lighted by the great bay of twenty-three lights, is filled with ancient Flemish glass, illustrating parts of Genesis and the Life of Christ.

The Hall, with its magnificent bay window and its ceiling, which is finely decorated with plaster work, is entered from the inner court and has an open timbered roof of the arch-braced type. The walls were hung with family portraits by Holbein, Janssens and Vandyck.

It is only natural that a house of this size has many apartments, enough to devote one to each separate use. So here is a 'candell house', and a 'candell chamber', and fifty other chambers varying in degree from the 'chiefe' or Queen's chamber, to one for the 'dayre mayd'. While in the extension formed by the wing on the right are the 'evidence' and 'still' rooms.

An extremely interesting thing about Hengrave is that many of the craftsmen's names are known, including the chief mason, joiner, carver and glazier. But who was the designer is not known.

John Sparke, freemason, received payment for the 'baye wyndowe in the parlor', or in other words, the oriel over the portal, which he roofed with half cupolas, wrought in ashlar. He is also thought to have created the equally fine bay in the hall. John Eustace made the East Anglian chimneys, with their rubbed brick shafts, Dyriche was the joiner, with Bartholomew as his servant; while John Birch was another, and Davy was the carver. Robert Watson acted as 'Ruler of the Building', for his name appears in the indenture. Neker was a joiner and responsible for doors, wainscoting, cupboards and fixed benches against the walls. He may also have made the roof.

The hall windows are full of fine glass, containing escutcheons. Some of this was painted for the house by Robert Wright, 'the glasyer' of Bury. Other came by purchases made locally or abroad.

It is not to be wondered that Queen Elizabeth paid this glorious house a visit. Indeed, she came twice in the time of the second Sir Thomas, and some of her letters, now in the State Papers Office, were addressed from 'the Court at Hengrave'. Thomas Kyston the second, was duly rewarded with a knighthood. An avenue is still known as Queen Elizabeth's Walk, and her room at the top of the great stairs is known as the Queen's Chamber. It is panelled to the ceiling and over the mantelpiece is a picture of Her Majesty.

The rooms have doorways of oak, bearing handles and locks of English design in steel, and are all named, inscribed with a scroll on the lintels, such as the 'Rose Chamber', 'Oriel Chamber', and the 'Wilbye Chamber'. This last is named after the celebrated madrigal composer John Wilbye (1574–1638), who spent most of his life here, holding the post of chief minstrel and confidential friend of the family. He was the third son of a tanner of Diss who possessed a lute, which he bequeathed to John. The Kytsons were great patrons of music and had a large collection of musical instruments which were housed in the minstrels' gallery. Wilbye remained in their service until the death of Lady Kytson in 1628. During this time his two sets of Madrigals were published, the one dated from Kytson's London home in Austin Friars, 1598; the second probably from Hengrave in 1609.

The first Sir Thomas did not enjoy the magnificence of Hengrave long, for he died in 1540. As he lay dying he was asked if Hengrave should not pass to his widow. 'Yes, marry shall she', was his reply, and she duly inherited. She became later the wife of Sir Richard Long of Shengay in Cambridgeshire; afterwards that of John Bourchier, Earl of Bath. In time Hengrave came to Earl Rivers, through whose issue it passed to Edward Gage, created a baronet by Charles II in 1632. It is alleged that a Sir W. Gage, introduced into this country, before 1725, the variety of plum that bears elsewhere the prefix, 'green', but is still known in Suffolk as a 'gage'.

The house contained many treasures, including a small mazer or grace cup, with a silver band, inscribed:

> Hold youre tunge and sey ye lest
> And let youre neyzbore sitte in rest
> Hoe so mayye god to blase
> Let hys neyzbore lyve in ese.

Within a living green enclosure is the ancient church of Hengrave, which has a round tower, though one of the more recent of this type. An old south porch was built by the Hengraves, who may also have rebuilt the fourteenth- or fifteenth-century church itself. For long this has been used as a mortuary chapel, and is now filled with old and faded renaissance tombs of the Kytsons, Rivers and Gages. A wall painting of St. Christopher that looked on at so much of history has departed with the damp.

Green shadows haunt Hengrave, a green reflection quivers in the lake, and silent shafts of light and memory fall from the traceried windows of the old shrine, across the effigies of those who once strode about those paths. Once upon a time they dallied in the gardens as laid out by the Dutchman gardener who was brought here from Norwich.

Flempton church, nearby, once had an epitaph to a former vicar, Blastus Godby. Note also the picturesque row of thatched cottages on the Green. Lackford church has a very fine font of the late thirteenth century, carved with foliage. It was only re-discovered in the middle of the last century, having been completely plastered over in Puritan times.

West Stow Hall is of very great interest and considerable age. It was a patrimony of Bury Abbey. At the Dissolution it was granted by Henry VIII to the Croftes' family, with whom it remained for many generations. Sir John Croftes made it his principal residence, and was responsible for the beautiful turreted gatehouse of thin red brick, now its main and charming feature. He had been a member of the household of Mary Tudor, Henry VIII's sister, and it is her arms that appear over the gateway. Mary and Charles Brandon, Duke of Suffolk, are reputed to have spent some of their time here.

Sir John died 1557, and was succeeded by his son, Edmund, who only survived his father a few days. Edmund's first wife was Elizabeth, daughter of Sir Thomas Kytson, the builder of Hen-grave. The issue failing, the Hall was bequeathed in 1669 to the Honourable Edward Progers, a terrible rascal. He died on 31st December 1772, aged 96, of the "anguish of cutting teeth, he having cut four new teeth and had several ready to cut, which so inflamed his gums that he died thereof".

The Hall is a fragment of what it was, although people living in the first half of the last century could remember a quadrangular court and extensive outbuildings, of which the fine old brick chimney of the Hall proper is the most distinguished survival. The moat was only filled in about the 'sixties of the last century.

The gatehouse, built in late Tudor times, is flanked by pro-jecting turrets, capped by dome-shaped brick roofs which support terra-cotta figures, while the crow-stepped gable is surmounted by such another figure. It is famous for its wall paintings in one of the Guard Rooms, done in black and red. On the return wall of the fireplace is a scene with sportsman, dogs and a pheasant in a flowery field. Over the chimney breast are depicted four of the Seven Ages of Man: 1, a youth hawking—"This doe I all the day"; 2, a young man making love—"This doe I while I may"; 3, a middle-aged man looking on at a the couple—"This did I when I might"; 4, an aged man—"Good Lord! will the world last for ever?" Above these are some beautiful dolphins and rose decorations, while the oak corner post is nicely carved.·

<u>Wordwell</u> has a Saxon church, the chancel of which is apsidal. The chief items of interest to the antiquary are the font, and the tympani of the ancient doorways. The outer, over the south, depicts unregenerate man; and the inner, over the north, the reformed and spiritual man made clean by baptism. This is denoted by water and an arm extended holding a ring, emblem of eternal life.

Ingham church has fragments of old glass including the crowned eagle with sceptre which was the badge of Anne Boleyn.

Culford once possessed a ford across the Lark. The Hall was built about 1591 by Sir Nicholas Bacon, and became the principal seat of the Marquis Cornwallis. It stands in about 500 acres of parkland, and has a barrow at the north. The gardens were famous as the home of the principal zonal geranium, such as 'Culford Rose' and 'E. R. Benyon'. The property was sold in 1934 and is now a school.

Ampton has been normally considered a part of the Livermeres, partaking of a common beauty in scenery of great parks, and a great sheet of water, the mere stretching into its boundaries. Besides the Hall, for long the residence of the Calthorpe family, it possesses an interesting little church, built of boulders, with stone dressings, and the most interesting part within is the Cocket Chantry, on the north side of the nave. This is entered beneath an obtuse pointed arch, the jambs and soffits of which are ornamented with bosses, between trefoil-headed panels. This little chantry was for long the family pew of Ampton Hall. Amongst the memorials is one to the foundress of the almshouses—'To the pious memory of Mrs. Dorothy Calthorpe:

A Virgin votary is oft in Snare,
This safely vow'd & made ye Poor her Heires.

The Royal Arms, dated 1661, are commented on by Munro Cautley:

At Ampton the Arms (Charles I) are of the greatest interest. They are cut out of wood about one inch thick in the form of fretwork, and the design except for a small part of the lion and one initial letter, is intact. Unfortunately, the colouring matter employed was distemper, and most of this has gone. There was a date on the small black overlapped by the point of the garter, which is believed to have been 1636, but the distemper was so loose on the wood that even a soft cloth would take it off, and too zealously dusting has destroyed this. Steps have been taken to get what colour is left, fixed. This achievement, 4 feet 6 inches high and 4 feet 3 inches wide, obviously stood on a former screen. Everything points to it being an early example, and flanking it are coloured and crowned badges, representing the Rose of England, and the Thistle of Scotland, fixed to iron spikes.

Ampton possesses a rare treasure in a copy of the Sealed Book, of which not more than thirty-one ever existed, and were allocated for the use of cathedrals and kindred churches. This was the result of the Savoy Conference, when the Prayer Book was revised about 1663, becoming the Convocation Prayer Book. An exact copy of it, altered by hand, was made on parchment and attached to the Carolean Act of Uniformity, of which it formed a part. This was called the 'Book Annexed', and they became known as the 'Sealed Books'. The Ampton copy is a folio, $15\frac{1}{2}$ inches by $10\frac{1}{4}$ inches, by $2\frac{1}{4}$ inches thick, but the first ten pages, including the title page, are missing. It was rebound in 1846 in white vellum, with an abundance of gold tooling.

It was said that Arthur Young was most eloquent about the beauties of Ampton and Livermere. Little Livermere church, now in ruins, stands alone in the park; the village which once surrounded it was removed outside the park in the course of beautification. It is now only used for funerals. The interior was made lovely with a ghostly imitation of vaulting in plaster and a parlour pew faces the three-decker. There was only one farm in the parish in 1879.

Great Livermere is on the eastern end of the park. A little east of the south porch is a small headstone inscribed: "Here lieth the body of William Sakings, he dide ye 28th of March, 1689, he was forkener [falconer] to King Charles ye 1st, King Charles ye 2nd, King James ye 2nd. Aged 78 years." The church had wall paintings of which only fragments survive, and a good fourteenth-century screen.

Capel Lofft, the sponsor of Bloomfield, lived at Troston in a small but very beautiful Elizabethan Hall, with some excellent plaster ceilings. The church has a great deal of interest with an excellent south porch, old glass, and three wall paintings of St. Christopher, St. George and the Dragon, and the martyrdom of St. Edmund. And there is a portion of a Doom over the chancel arch.

Honington, birthplace of Robert Bloomfield the Suffolk poet and author of the "Farmer's Boy", is not far from:

> Where noble Grafton spreads her rich domain
> Round Euston's water'd vale, and sloping plain.

His father, the village tailor, died of the smallpox before his son was a year old. Of the same stock derived Charles James Bloomfield, Bishop of London.

The cottage by the church is still there, now brick cased with a pantiled roof. The only education the poet received was from his mother, who started a little school on the death of her husband. It ended when she married again. He also received assistance from a kindly disposed schoolmaster at Ixworth, who taught him to write; otherwise he was self-taught.

He commenced life working on the land for his uncle William Austin of Sapiston, and this kind of life he has immortalized in his verse with graphic accuracy, inspired largely by Thomson's *Seasons*. Proving weakly in health he went to London to join his brother George, who was a shoemaker, and was apprenticed to the same master. His arrival in London is described by his brother—"I have in my mind's eye a little boy, not bigger than boys generally are at 12 years old [he was 14½]. When I met him and his mother at the inn he strutted before us, dressed just as he came from keeping sheep and hogs—his shoes filled full of stumps in the heels. Looking about him, he slipt up—his nails were unused to a flat pavement."

His own record of the journey was: "Now the strict truth of the case is this—that I came in my Sunday clothes, such as they were; for I remember well selling my smock frock for a shilling, and slyly washing my best hat in the horse yard to give it a gloss fit to appear in the meridian of London."

Later, he married the daughter of a Woolwich boat-builder and when housekeeping in a single room in Bell Alley, Coleman Street, he composed the stanzas of the 'Farmer's Boy', much of which he memorized before committing to paper. Capel Lofft, squire of Troston, took him under his wing, and was instrumental in getting the poem published. Within three years of its appearance 26,000 copies were sold, and it was translated into Latin, Italian and French.

Bloomfield was considered too rustic by the literati of his day. Lamb disliked him, but then he hated Lofft more, whose initials were apt to be taken for his own. Byron spoke of Bloomfield as a "tuneful cobbler" and Lofft as "a kind of gratis accoucheur to those who wish to be delivered of rhyme, but do not know how to bring forth". On the other hand, Hazlitt said—"as a painter of simple natural scenery, and of still life of the country, few writers have more undeniable and unassuming pretensions".

The church at Honington derives from Norman times, with a south doorway of that period, and a chancel arch of the same. The communion table is of the Stuart period, also the altar rails and some old benches, on one of which is a bagpiper and a unicorn. On the south wall is an early painting of the story of St. Nicholas. The wicked landlord and his wife are seen killing the three boys in bed, who came to their inn and St. Nicholas is raising them.

In the summer of 1802, Bloomfield walked from Sapiston to Thetford passing Euston Hall on the way. In his poem, "Barnham Water", he alludes to the one small streamlet that crossed the way. This nameless stream that unites with the Little Ouse west of the village has been widened and an ornamental bridge thrown across it. W. G. Clarke says: "In the great frost of 1814, a flock of sheep crossed safely on the ice, the shepherd watching the while with the upmost trepidation." The church of Sapiston is chiefly remarkable for its very fine Norman south doorway. One fifteenth-century bell is inscribed—"May the joys of light be ours by the merits of Thomas."

Great Fakenham church is mostly fourteenth century with a ring handle on the door, the boss of which forms a mask. Here the ghost walked.

Euston parish has a length of six miles, there is a bridge over the Ouse, and for a mile the road is known as The Deal Row. In Euston Park, John Evelyn had a hand in planting the trees for Lord Arlington in 1671.

Euston is one of the prettiest villages in Suffolk, and the huge cedars near the park gates add picturesqueness to the landscape. Or as Clarke has it—"The ancient, low parapeted stone bridge, the magnificent oaks, beech, lime and elms, the quaint lath-and-plaster dwellings embowered in creepers, and the village green all help to form a pleasant picture which is the stranger's impression of Euston. Its present aspect is the result of over 200 years' planning, pruning and preservation."

According to Evelyn the estate was sold by Sir T. Rookwood to Sir Henry Bennett, who in 1663 was made Earl of Arlington and Viscount Thetford. He built Euston Hall about 1670 and some of the present building dates from that time. His only daughter was married to the Earl of Euston, who afterwards became the first Duke of Grafton. She was 12 and he 15. His mother was the beautiful and notorious Barbara Castlemaine and his father the King.

The pedestal of the boundary cross on Barnham Common is hollow and sometimes contains water. It is alleged that once when a plague raged in Thetford, travellers to and from had to wash their money in this basin. One of the most remarkable of the barrows was opened, which contained at least ten Bronze Age urns, one of the Early Iron Age and one of the first century A.D.

Elvedon Hall was built in 1870 for the late Maharajah Duleep Singh who had purchased the estate in 1863. He once possessed the Koh-i-noor diamond which he gave to Queen Victoria. There was a movement afoot recently to have his body taken back to India for burning as, according to Sikh ritual, the dead should be cremated and not buried. He lived here in oriental splendour and became a Christian. He was also well versed in local archaeology and adopted the role of an English squire. His simple grave eastwards of the church is in contrast with the elaborate tomb he had erected for his guardian, Sir Spencer Login, in Felixstowe churchyard.

The church has been rebuilt in a most costly and elaborate manner; while, facing the Hall, the seat of Lord Iveagh, a flint and stone-built tower and lengthy stone cloister leads to the south door. This, in no known style of architecture, can only be considered as a folly.

Santon Downham is a beautiful little place with a tiny Norman church. It has a curious piece of sculpture over the south door, that may be a paschal lamb. The sandy soil here has always been subject to storms but conifers have made the soil firm. For many years the vicar was an old friend of mine, the Reverend H. Tyrrell Green, who served in the First War as a private and was badly wounded during the March 1918 retreat. He was noted for his brass rubbings. There is a stained glass window, depicting St. Francis among Breckland birds. "Be Thou praised my Lord for all Thy creatures."

Brandon is a town and rather outside the scope of this book, but one wonders what has replaced the two main industries of rabbit fur and flint knapping, both of which have been carried on for centuries. It has been described as a town of flint houses and walls, flint chapels, flint roads, flint chip stacks and flint knappers. One could identify the natives by the gaudiness of their clothes. Dyer and Snare were local names. This is the centre of the Breck district.

Wangford Hall, now a farmhouse, was once the residence of Sir Robert Wright, Lord Chief Justice of the Common Pleas and King's Bench. He presided at the trial of the Seven Bishops and died in 1689. The church, much restored, is dedicated to St. Denis. This was a great centre for rabbits.

There is a tradition that a tunnel under the fens runs from Lakenheath to Ely and that it has oak sides and roof. It was used in the time of Hereward. This was a great place for prehistoric remains.

Lakenheath church is full of interest and Cautley gives a lengthy description. He thinks the lower part of the tower was a Galilee porch and in its upper a chantry chapel. It has a splendid nave roof and some quite remarkable bench-ends, with figures which include a contortionist, tiger and looking-glass, and a unicorn. The thirteenth-century font is the best in the county, with many wall paintings. A medieval bell has the unusual inscription—"May Christ always give us a joyful life."

Lakenheath is now a large U.S.A.F. base, and Princess Anne opened a new £900,000 school for American children in June, 1970. Once upon a time each householder from surrounding districts had to make a journey of 14 miles to Lakenheath and spend a day catching eels for the cellarer.

Eriswell is in the Lark valley, extending westwards to the fens and northwards to Lakenheath. On the north side of the parish, near the Hall, was a chapel dedicated to St. Lawrence, the remains of which in 1879 were a dovecote. The church is practically fourteenth century throughout.

Mildenhall is a town and the largest parish in the county, extending to 17,000 acres, half of which was once fen and mere. It is built on the site of a settlement of the Stone Age, and is one of the few places where a Market Cross survives. Kirby says, "Towards the fens are several large streets as big as ordinary towns, called by the inhabitants, Rows: as West Row, Beck Row and Holywell Row". It was at West Row where a ploughman turned up the Roman silver plate now housed in the British Museum. When I was there I met the man who had ploughed over the spot for many a year; the treasure was not discovered until a tractor plough, ploughing that much deeper, was used. He was very sick at having missed it.

Not far removed from Mildenhall, at Bargate Farm, on the north bank of the Lark, was located the site of the Anglo-Saxon Council of Clovesho.

Worlington church contains one of the earliest bells in Suffolk, dating from the earlier years of the fourteenth century and inscribed—"Johannes Godynge de Lenne me fecit". There is a good deal of interest in this old building.

Freckenham, a large village of some 2,500 acres, extends from the Lark near Judes Ferry southwards to Herringswell, and was once a place of no small importance. Exactly opposite the Hall, on the north of the road in Mount Meadow, is a chalk mound, called locally The Castle. A subterranean passage is said to run from this to the Hall. Here was a residence of the bishops of Rochester, and the reason that Kentish influence extends thus far is probably because of Anna's eldest daughter's marriage with the Kentish King Eorconbeorht about 640. (This may explain other associations with Rochester in the county, such as the Priory at Felixstowe.) Here stayed William the Conqueror's physician when on his way to cure (or kill) the Abbot of Bury. In the wall of the north aisle of the church is an interesting, though defaced, alabaster reredos, retaining some of its old colour. This was discovered in 1776, fixed face to wall, and illustrates the curious legend of St. Elegius, who became the patron saint of blacksmiths. On one occasion a horse was brought to him that would not allow itself to be shod. The saint, nothing daunted, took off the animal's leg, shod it and then restored it to the horse.

Barton Mills, which is separated from Mildenhall by the Lark, has a considerable amount of old glass in the church windows. But what interests me is the small charity that was once distributed by the wealthy rector and churchwardens to the poor on St. Stephen's Day (when they hunted the wren), Christmas Day and Easter Sunday. How good to the poor were these clerics in fat livings! The inn is the Dog and Partridge.

Tuddenham St. Mary's church is mostly of the fourteenth-century, and the parish was noted for certain wild flowers of the steppe species, such as the fingered speedwell and the rupture wort.

And so on to Icklingham which was a Roman station, with a Roman cemetery and a house of that period, together with a number of earthworks. It is not surprising therefore to find that here was one of the ghosts of the headless variety, lightly clad, riding a horse, to be seen galloping over the low meadows by the river at Temple Bridge. He may have been old Sir John de Cambridge, one time prior of Bury, who was executed by the same mob that disposed of Sir John Cavendish.

The church of All Saints, which is of Norman origin, witness two blocked-up windows of that period, principally dates from the fourteenth century. Architectural features apart, of which there are many, the church holds much of interest, chiefly in the encaustic tiles which pave the chancel. One at least bears a Gothic canopy, others faces or heraldic devices. They evidently derive from the fourteenth century and compare with similar specimens at Ely, St. Albans and Hertford.

There are remains of the screen, which in this case is distinguished by the huge sill, $10\frac{1}{2}$ inches high, that runs right across the portal, providing a step. The Jacobean pulpit is very fine, with notable turned balusters, hand rail and steps. The altar rails are of the same period, while there are old benches made from riven chestnut planks, with fleurs-de-lis poppy heads. A good deal of old glass remains in the windows, some of which was found by an old sexton named Henry Naylor. He was digging on the north side, near the chancel, when he unearthed "sufficient to fill a peck measure".

But the chief glory of the little church is the magnificent chest, covered with wrought-iron scroll work, considered to be the finest in existence. Here, too, are early examples of hassocks, formed by solid tussocks of reeds. It should be noted also that the reed thatch of the chancel roof was, and maybe still is, plaited on the underside to avoid the necessity of wood battens—further evidence of an improvisation on the part of a country craftsman.

In 1556 "John Thompson, rector, bequeathed to the poor and others being present at his funeral, nine shillings in beer, bread and cheese. Also at his month's mind there be baked a combe of rye and brewed a comb of malt and half a quarter of these to be bought for the relief of the poor and others being present."

It is interesting to note instances of common origin and workmanship in the building of these churches. The tower of Icklingham St. James was built by the same master mason as that of Flempton. Both of these towers fell about the same time at the beginning of the nineteenth century.

There is another legend in Icklingham around a bit of a hillock known as 'Deadman's Grave'. It is said that here a man with a horse who met a sudden death lies buried, and in retaliation for neglect of a Christian burial, his spirit frightens all horses and other animals that pass this way after dusk.

Herringswell church has the distinction of being dedicated to St. Ethelbert, the King of East Anglia, who was beheaded by Offa, King of the Mercians, in 792. It was destroyed by fire on Sunday, the 28th February 1869, during the morning service; caused by the over-heating of a chimney pipe passing through the roof. The distinguishing feature is the tower, where the south, north and east walls are supported by arches on detached columns.

The Ichnield Way enters Breckland at Cavenham, between which and Lackford Bridge the track is over Cavenham Heath, where there are two lines of Black Ditches. Prehistoric implements and particular chalkland flowers are to be found here.

Postscript

We have come to the end of our excursion. It is a record which hardly any other county can offer. The story of an inheritance passed on and down, almost inviolate, through all the years. Can it continue in this world of change and disregard of old chivalry? There is hope it may, remembering this is England. Therefore we might close with the words of Vita Sackville West:

> Tang of the reeking byres,
> Land of the English breed,
> A man and his land makes a man and his creed.

Index

Trevelyan, G. M., 13, 15
Trimley St. Martin, 83
Trimley St. Mary, 83
Troston, 177
Tuddenham St. Martin, 81
Tuddenham St. Mary, 182
Tunstall, 76
Turner, J. Doman, 62
——— John, 108
Tyrell, Sir James, 107

U

Ubbeston, 111
Ufford, Robert de, 79
Ufford, 79

V

Victoria, Queen, 13

W

Walberswick, 58–62
Waldringfield, 82
Walpole, 48
Walsham-le-Willows, 19, 163
Wangford, 44
Wantisden, 79–80
Washbrook, 89
Wattisfield, 165
Waveney, River, 16, 27, 41
Wenhaston, 20, 49
Wentworth, Lady Anne, 32
Wentworth family, the, 31
West Creeting see Creeting St.
  Peter (West Creeting)
Westhorpe, 117
Westerfield, 101
Westhall, 42
Westleton, 25, 52
Westmoreland, Earl of, 71
Weston Hall, 38
West Stow, 174

Wetheringsett, 108
Whatfield, 146
Whepstead, 19, 142
Wherstead, 85–6
Whistlecraft, Orlando, 108
White, William, 22
Wickhambrook, 19, 139
Wickham Market, 77
Wilby, 111
Willoughby, Sir Christopher, 73
Willoughby of Eresby and Parham,
  Peregrine, Lord, 73
Wingfield, Sir John, 114
——— Katherine, 114
Wingfield Castle, 114
Wingfield family, the, 113–5
Wint, Peter de, 62
Winthrop, John, 128
Wissett, 113
Wissington, 125
Withersfield, 137
Wolsey, Cardinal, 42, 51
Women's Institutes, 22
Woodbridge School, 81
Woolpit, 159–60
Woolsey, John, 32
Woolverstone, 85, 98
Wordwell, 175
Worlingham, 38
Worlington, 181
Worlingworth, 109
Wrentham, 44
Wyatville, Sir Jeffrey, 85

Y

Yarmouth, 17, 49
Yaxley, 116
Young, Arthur, 16, 176
Yox, River, 51
Yoxford, 20, 50–51
Ypres, 17

Z

Zincke, F. Barham, 85–6